STECK-VAUGHN

SO-CFE-477

Target
SPELLING 540

Margaret Scarborough
Mary F. Brigham
Teresa A. Miller

STECK-VAUGHN
ELEMENTARY · SECONDARY · ADULT · LIBRARY

A Harcourt Company

www.steck-vaughn.com

Table of Contents

Acknowledgments

Editorial Director:	Stephanie Muller
Editor:	Kathleen Gower Wiseman
Associate Director of Design:	Cynthia Ellis
Design Managers:	Sheryl Cota, Katie Nott
Illustrators:	Peg Dougherty, Jimmy Longacre, Cindy Aarvig, David Griffin, Lynn McClain
Cover Design:	Bassett & Brush Design, Todd Disrud and Stephanie Schreiber

ISBN 0-7398-2458-9
Copyright ©2001 Steck-Vaughn Company
All rights reserved. No part of the material protected by this copyright may be reproduced or utilized in any form or by any means, electronic or mechanical, including photocopying, recording, or by any information storage and retrieval system, without permission in writing from the copyright owner. Requests for permission to make copies of any part of the work should be mailed to: Copyright Permissions, Steck-Vaughn Company, P.O. Box 26015, Austin, TX 78755. Printed in the United States of America.

1 2 3 4 5 6 7 8 9 DBH 04 03 02 01 00

Word Study Plan

1 **LOOK** at the word. _____

2 **SAY** the word. _____

3 **THINK** about each letter. _____

4 **SPELL** the word aloud. _____

5 **WRITE** the word. _____

6 **CHECK** the spelling. _____

7 **REPEAT** the steps
if you need more practice. _____

© 2001 Steck-Vaughn Company. All Rights Reserved.

Name _____

Spelling Strategies

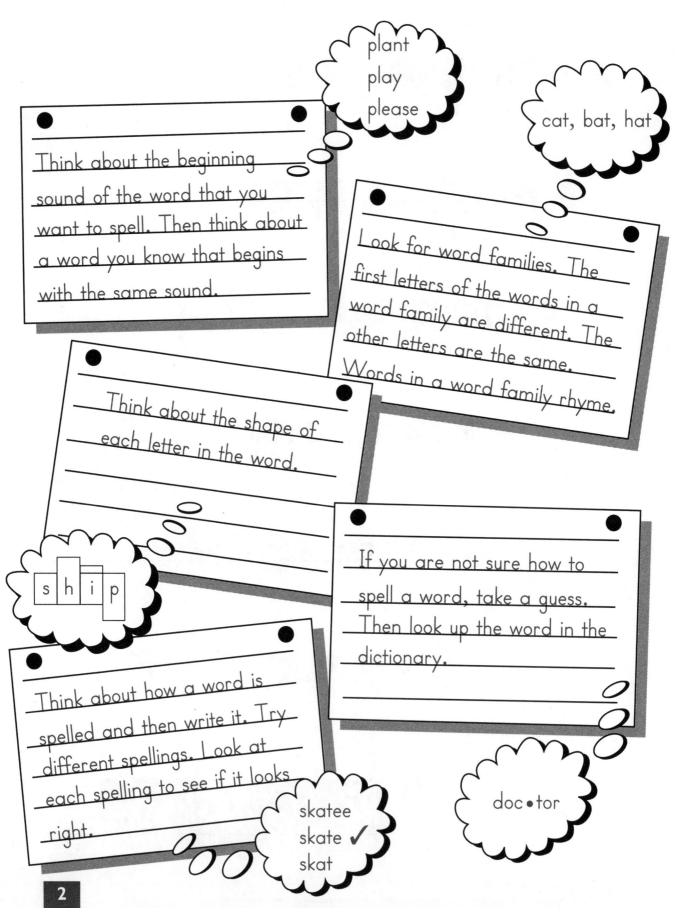

plant
play
please

cat, bat, hat

Think about the beginning sound of the word that you want to spell. Then think about a word you know that begins with the same sound.

Look for word families. The first letters of the words in a word family are different. The other letters are the same. Words in a word family rhyme.

Think about the shape of each letter in the word.

s h i p

If you are not sure how to spell a word, take a guess. Then look up the word in the dictionary.

Think about how a word is spelled and then write it. Try different spellings. Look at each spelling to see if it looks right.

skatee
skate ✓
skat

doc•tor

DAY 1

Words with *ee*

bee	**feet**	**once**
free	**meet**	**your**

A Circle the spelling word. Then write it on the line.

1. Can you (meet) me at the mall? ___ meet ___

2. I was stung by a bee. _____

3. We go to the store once a week. _____

4. My friend won a free prize. _____

5. My feet are bigger than my sister's! _____

6. Will you lend me your pencil? _____

B Circle the word that is the same as the top one.

free	once	meet	bee	your	feet
(free)	ouce	mect	bic	yoor	feef
fere	oncc	mcct	dee	youn	feet
feer	once	meef	bee	yonr	teef
frea	onec	meet	bec	your	fect

C Write a spelling word under each picture.

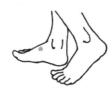

1. _____   2. _____   3. _____

© 2001 Steck-Vaughn Company. All Rights Reserved.

Name _____

Lesson 1 — Words with *ee*

bee	feet	once
free	meet	your

A Fill in the boxes with the correct spelling words.

1. f r e e

2. ☐☐☐☐

3. ☐☐☐☐

4. ☐☐☐☐

5. ☐☐☐☐

6. ☐☐☐

B Fill in each blank with a spelling word.

1. A _____bee_____ likes to land on flowers.

2. His _____ had grown since last year.

3. Many stories begin, "_____ upon a time."

4. I like to _____ my friends for lunch.

5. Air is _____ for everyone.

6. Please raise _____ hand before you speak.

C Find the missing letters. Then write the word.

1. f _____ _____ t   _____

2. m e _____ _____   _____

3. b _____ e   _____

4

Words with *ee*

bee	feet	once
free	meet	your

A Use the correct spelling words to complete the story.

The boy was playing outside on a hot summer day. He

was so glad to be _____ of school. Now he had lots

of time to _____ his friends and play all kinds of

games outdoors. One of his favorite games was tag.

He took off his shoes. His _____ were bare. He

ran past a tree. Suddenly, he felt a sharp pain in one foot. A

_____ had stung him!

B Write the two pairs of spelling words that rhyme.

1. _____   _____

2. _____   _____

C Put an *X* on the word that is <u>not</u> the same.

1.	feet	feet	~~feet~~	feet	feet
2.	once	once	once	once	onec
3.	free	free	free	tree	free
4.	bee	bec	bee	bee	bee
5.	meet	meet	meat	meet	meet

© 2001 Steck-Vaughn Company. All Rights Reserved.

Name _____

Words with *ee*

bee	feet	once
free	meet	your

A Write the spelling words that have the *ee* pattern.

bee _____ _____ _____

B Write the spelling words in ABC order.

1. bee　　2. feet　　3. _____

4. _____　　5. _____　　6. _____

C Write each spelling word three times in cursive.

bee _____

free _____

feet _____

your _____

once _____

meet _____

D Complete each sentence.

1. I would like to <u>meet</u> _____.

2. My <u>feet</u> are _____.

3. I want to be <u>free</u> to _____.

4. <u>Once</u> upon a time, _____.

Words with *ea*

peach	clean	read
heat	beans	give

A **Circle the spelling word. Then write it on the line.**

1. We'll turn on the heat when it's cold. _____

2. I have to clean my room before I leave. _____

3. My favorite fruit is a peach. _____

4. I will give you a birthday present. _____

5. Did you read about the flood yesterday? _____

6. We ate soup with beans last night. _____

B **Write the spelling words in ABC order.**

1. _____   2. _____   3. _____

4. _____   5. _____   6. _____

C **Circle the word that is the same as the top one.**

read	beans	give	clean	heat	peach
nead	beans	givc	clear	beat	peaoh
reed	deans	qive	clean	heet	peech
reab	beanz	give	cleon	heat	peaeh
read	beens	dive	elean	haet	peach

D **Circle the letters that are the same in each spelling word.**

peach   heat   clean   beans   read

© 2001 Steck-Vaughn Company. All Rights Reserved.

Name _____

Lesson 2

Words with *ea*

peach	clean	read
heat	beans	give

A Fill in the boxes with the correct spelling words.

1.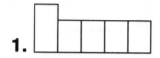

2.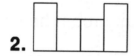

3.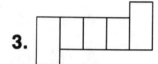

4.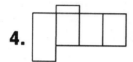

5.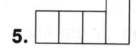

6.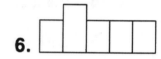

B Fill in each blank with a spelling word.

1. I like to _____ a book on a rainy day.

2. Let me _____ you the key to the house.

3. That's the best _____ I've ever eaten.

4. One of my favorite vegetables is fresh green _____.

5. If you make a mess, you should _____ it up.

6. Let's _____ the food so we can eat.

C Find the missing letters. Then write the word.

1. h ____ ____ ____   _____

2. ____ ____ ____ d   _____

3. ____ ____ ____ c h   _____

8

Words with *ea*

peach	clean	read
heat	beans	give

A Use the correct spelling words to complete the story.

I love summer. Some of the best things about summer are
fresh vegetables and fruits. When you're hot, a cold, sweet

_____ tastes great. I like to go to the market and

pick out the biggest one I can find. I _____ the

cashier my money and then take the fruit home. I wash it to

make sure it's _____.

My mother has a garden in our back yard. In summer we

have fresh corn, _____, and peas. She is always

working in the garden. I don't like to work in the garden. My

back gets tired from bending over. I would much rather

_____ a book.

B Write the spelling word that names something you can eat.

<u>peach</u> _____

C Complete each sentence.

1. I like to <u>give</u> _____.

2. I don't like to <u>clean</u> _____.

3. Sometimes I <u>read</u> _____.

Name _____

© 2001 Steck-Vaughn Company. All Rights Reserved.

Lesson 2

Words with *ea*

peach	clean	read
heat	beans	give

A Write the spelling words that have the *ea* pattern.

_____ _____ _____

_____ _____

B Put an **X** on the word that is <u>not</u> the same.

1.	beans	beans	beans	deans	beans
2.	read	read	reab	read	read
3.	clean	clean	clean	clean	clear
4.	heat	heaf	heat	heat	heat
5.	give	give	give	qive	give
6.	peach	peach	peack	peach	peach

C Write each spelling word three times in cursive.

clean _____

give _____

beans _____

read _____

peach _____

heat _____

10

Words with -*aw* and -*ow*

law	how	clown
draw	plow	frown

A Circle the spelling word. Then write it on the line.

1. When you feel upset, you may frown. _____

2. You must use a plow before you plant. _____

3. The law says you must stop at red lights. _____

4. Please tell me how you did that. _____

5. The clown wore a lot of makeup. _____

6. Can you draw animals? _____

B Circle the word that is the same as the top one.

law	draw	how	plow	clown	frown
low	drow	low	plow	clawn	frown
law	drav	haw	plaw	clowm	frawn
lav	draw	how	phow	clown	frowm
luw	braw	hov	phou	clomn	forwn

C Fill in the boxes with the correct spelling words.

1. 2. 3.

© 2001 Steck-Vaughn Company. All Rights Reserved.

Name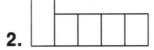

11

Words with -*aw* and -*ow*

law	how	clown
draw	plow	frown

A Write the spelling words in ABC order.

1. _____ 2. _____ 3. _____

4. _____ 5. _____ 6. _____

B Write the spelling words that have the *ow* pattern.

_____ _____ _____ _____

C Put an *X* on the word that is <u>not</u> the same.

1. draw	draw	draw	darw	draw
2. plow	plow	plow	glow	plow
3. clown	clown	clonw	clown	clown
4. frown	frown	frown	frown	frowm

D Write the three pairs of spelling words that rhyme.

1. _____ _____

2. _____ _____

3. _____ _____

E Circle the letters that are the same in each spelling word.

clown   frown   how   plow

Lesson 3

Words with -*aw* and -*ow*

law	how	clown
draw	plow	frown

A Use the correct spelling words to complete the story.

My dad wanted to teach me _____ to plant a crop

of corn. I had never planted a crop before, so I was a little

nervous. I must have had a _____ on my face because

my dad told me not to worry. He said everything would be fine.

I knew that we would have to dig up the soil before we planted

the seeds, but I wasn't sure what to use. I asked my dad, and he

said we would need a _____. "What does it look like?" I

asked him. "I'll _____ you a picture of it," he told me.

B Find each hidden word from the list.

peach	beans	straw	down	plow	again
heat	read	draw	frown	how	could
feast	meat	law	clown	cow	every

```
f  r  e  a  d  i  f  l  a  w  i  f  e  a  s  t  f
b  a  t  b  r  e  i  c  g  f  i  e  w  o  r  i  e
i  f  b  e  a  n  s  o  a  m  u  c  p  a  h  e  s
v  t  c  e  w  m  k  u  i  t  r  l  e  m  e  a  t
e  e  v  e  r  y  n  l  n  o  c  o  a  n  a  l  r
f  r  e  e  a  x  o  d  p  l  o  w  c  i  t  m  a
h  o  w  f  r  o  w  n  d  o  w  n  h  o  t  r  w
```

Name _____

© 2001 Steck-Vaughn Company. All Rights Reserved.

13

DAY 4

law	how	clown
draw	plow	frown

A Fill in each blank with a spelling word.

1. The farmer will _____ the fields in May.

2. Do you know _____ to use the camera?

3. She likes to _____ pictures of her family.

4. The _____ works at the circus.

5. It is against the _____ to steal.

6. The _____ on his face means he is not happy.

B Write each spelling word three times in cursive.

draw _____

clown _____

how _____

law _____

plow _____

frown _____

C Write a spelling word under each picture.

1. _____   2. _____   3. _____

Words with *-oi* and *-oy*

DAY 1

oil	coin	joy
spoil	join	toy

A Circle the spelling word. Then write it on the line.

1. Milk will spoil if it's not kept cold. _____

2. Joy is what you feel when you're happy. _____

3. Would you like to join our band? _____

4. His favorite coin was the 1905 nickel. _____

5. Her mom changes the oil in their car. _____

6. The toy poodle is a small dog. _____

B Find the missing letters. Then write the word.

1. ____ i ____   _____

2. t ____ ____   _____

3. j ____ ____ n   _____

C Write the spelling words in ABC order.

1. _____   2. _____   3. _____

4. _____   5. _____   6. _____

D Circle the letters that are the same in each spelling word.

oil   spoil   coin   join

© 2001 Steck-Vaughn Company. All Rights Reserved.

Name _____

15

Words with *-oi* and *-oy*

oil	coin	joy
spoil	join	toy

A Fill in the boxes with the correct spelling words.

1.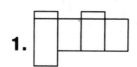

2.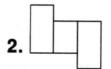

3.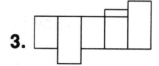

4.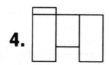

5.

6.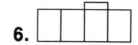

B Circle the word that is the same as the top one.

spoil	joy	coin	oil	toy	join
sqoil	jov	coir	oil	foy	joir
spiol	jey	coin	oel	tov	join
spoil	ioy	cion	ool	toi	joyn
sgoil	joy	coiu	oit	toy	jojn

C Write the spelling words that have the *oi* pattern.

_____ _____ _____ _____

D Write the spelling word that names a feeling.

_____

Words with *-oi* and *-oy*

DAY 3

oil	coin	joy
spoil	join	toy

A Use the correct spelling words to complete the story.

A boy went to the mountains to wait for his birthday picnic

to begin. But it looked like it might rain. He rubbed the gold

_____ in his pocket for good luck. He didn't want rain

to _____ his birthday.

His friends would _____ the party in an hour. Oh,

the _____ of being in the woods! First, they would

hike and then eat a big lunch. Later, they would have cake for

dessert, and he would open his birthday presents.

B Circle each spelling word that is hidden in the big word.
Write the word on the line.

1. spoiled _____

2. soil _____

3. joyful _____

4. joined _____

C Fill in each blank with a spelling word.

1. Visiting with my friends brings me _____.

2. Some people like to _____ clubs.

3. His favorite _____ is the stuffed bear.

4. _____ will float on top of water.

© 2001 Steck-Vaughn Company. All Rights Reserved.

Name _____

17

Lesson 4

Words with *-oi* and *-oy*

oil	coin	joy
spoil	join	toy

A Answer each question with a spelling word.

1. Which word means "a piece of money"? _____

2. Which word means "happiness"? _____

3. Which word means "to get together"? _____

4. Which word means "something to play with"? _____

5. Which word means "a greasy liquid"? _____

B Write each spelling word three times in cursive.

join _____

joy _____

coin _____

oil _____

toy _____

spoil _____

C Complete each sentence.

1. Joy is _____.

2. I would like to join _____.

3. My favorite toy is _____.

4. You need a coin to _____.

18

DAY 1

Words with *ou*

scout	cloud	ground
trout	proud	pound

A Circle the spelling word. Then write it on the line.

1. He felt proud when his sister won. _____

2. We buy ground beef for hamburgers. _____

3. There was not a cloud in the sky today. _____

4. I like to fish for trout. _____

5. We buy chicken by the pound at the store. _____

6. Can you scout around for some firewood? _____

B Find the missing letters. Then write the word.

1. ____ r ____ ____ n ____   _____

2. t ____ ____ ____ t   _____

3. ____ r ____ ____ d   _____

C Match each word with its picture. Then write the word.

1. trout   _____

2. cloud   _____

3. ground   _____

© 2001 Steck-Vaughn Company. All Rights Reserved.

Name _____

Words with *ou*

scout	cloud	ground
trout	proud	pound

A Write the three pairs of spelling words that rhyme.

1. _____ _____

2. _____ _____

3. _____ _____

B Put an *X* on the word that is <u>not</u> the same.

1.	trout	trout	trout	trout	trouf
2.	pound	pound	pouud	pound	pound
3.	cloud	cloud	cloud	cloub	cloud
4.	scout	scouf	scout	scout	scout
5.	ground	ground	ground	ground	gruond

C Write the spelling words in ABC order.

1. _____ 2. _____ 3. _____

4. _____ 5. _____ 6. _____

D Fill in the boxes with the correct spelling words.

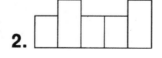

1. _____ 2. _____ 3. _____

Lesson 5

Words with *ou*

scout	cloud	ground
trout	proud	pound

A Find each hidden word from the list.

ground	mound	hound	proud	shout	about
found	sound	bound	cloud	out	scout
pound	wound	round	loud	clout	trout

a	g	r	o	u	n	d	o	n	p	r	o	u	d	o	u
o	h	o	u	n	d	l	o	u	o	u	m	h	w	a	s
w	o	u	n	d	o	u	f	o	u	n	o	v	h	s	h
h	w	t	c	a	v	r	o	u	n	d	u	t	e	o	o
e	h	o	l	b	l	o	u	d	d	o	n	r	n	u	u
r	o	u	o	o	u	t	l	o	u	t	d	o	u	n	t
e	v	e	u	u	i	w	e	r	e	f	o	u	n	d	c
l	o	w	d	t	u	o	d	s	c	o	u	t	o	u	l
o	b	o	u	n	d	w	h	y	c	l	o	u	t	t	o

B Use the correct spelling words to complete the story.

We went camping in the woods for one week. First, we

set the tent up on soft _____. It didn't take long to

_____ the tent stakes into the earth. Later, we

walked to a pond to fish for _____.

C Circle the letters that are the same in each spelling word.

scout   trout   ground   pound   cloud   proud

Name _____

21

© 2001 Steck-Vaughn Company. All Rights Reserved.

Words with *ou*

scout	cloud	ground
trout	proud	pound

A Circle the word that is the same as the top one.

scout	trout	ground	pound	cloud	proud
scuot	troul	gronud	paund	clond	proub
scoul	frout	ground	pounb	cloub	proud
scout	truot	groumd	dounp	cloud	porud
scont	trout	qround	pound	clowd	droup

B Answer each question with a spelling word.

1. Which word is a kind of fish? _____

2. Which word can mean "to hit something hard"? _____

3. Which word can mean "to look around"? _____

4. Which word can mean "earth"? _____

C Write each spelling word three times in cursive.

ground _____

cloud _____

proud _____

pound _____

scout _____

trout _____

Review

bee	peach	how
free	heat	plow
feet	clean	clown
meet	beans	frown
once	read	give

A Write a spelling word under each picture.

1. _____ 2. _____ 3. _____

        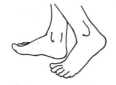

4. _____ 5. _____ 6. _____

B Fill in each blank with a spelling word.

1. Can you _____ me change for a dollar?

2. _____ much did that peach cost?

3. The _____ from the fireplace warmed the room.

4. Are you _____ to visit with me tomorrow?

5. We meet _____ a week for lunch.

6. My sister helped me _____ the kitchen.

7. Please _____ me outside at five o'clock.

© 2001 Steck-Vaughn Company. All Rights Reserved.

Name _____

law	oil	cloud
draw	spoil	proud
joy	coin	ground
toy	join	pound
your	scout	trout

C **Write the spelling word that rhymes with the word pair.**

1. about   trout   _____

2. pound   sound   _____

3. aloud   cloud   _____

4. boy   joy   _____

5. straw   draw   _____

6. oil   boil   _____

D **Use the correct spelling words to complete the story.**

How do you feel about art? Do you like to _____?

Are _____ fingers always looking for a pencil or pen?

I'm always drawing pictures in my spare time. My favorite

things to draw are outside. Once I drew a _____ in the

sky and a tree on a hill. When I was up in the mountains, I

drew a _____ in a clear stream. Maybe someday I will

_____ an art class. I might want to make my living by

drawing pictures for other people.

Words with *ea*

real	beak	dream
deal	speak	leap

A Circle the spelling word. Then write it on the line.

1. Try to leap over the puddle. _____

2. The bird's beak is bright orange. _____

3. A deal can mean an agreement. _____

4. Will you speak to the group today? _____

5. I had a funny dream last night. _____

6. Do you like the taste of real butter? _____

B Fill in each blank with a spelling word.

1. She tries to _____ over the waves in the ocean.

2. When you _____, your voice is soft and clear.

3. The price for the radio is a great _____.

4. I like _____ maple syrup on pancakes.

5. He hopes his _____ will come true.

6. The woodpecker uses its _____ to get food.

C Write the spelling words in ABC order.

1. _____   2. _____   3. _____

4. _____   5. _____   6. _____

© 2001 Steck-Vaughn Company. All Rights Reserved.

Name _____

Words with *ea*

real	beak	dream
deal	speak	leap

A Write the spelling word that rhymes with the word pair.

1. steal   deal   _____

2. steam   cream   _____

3. speak   streak   _____

B Find the missing letters. Then write the word.

1. ____ ____ ____ ____ k   _____

2. d ____ ____ ____   _____

3. l ____ ____ ____   _____

C Circle the letters that are the same in each spelling word.

real   deal   speak   beak   dream   leap

D Match each picture with its word. Then write the word.

1. dream   _____

2. leap   _____

3. beak   _____

Lesson 6

Words with *ea*

real	beak	dream
deal	speak	leap

A Use the correct spelling words to complete the story.

One night it was raining hard when I went to bed.

The wind blew through the trees and made odd noises.

I had a strange _____. My sister was trying to

_____ to me, but her voice sounded different. I

woke up and knew the dream wasn't _____. My

sister was asleep in her bed.

B Put an *X* on the word that is **not** the same.

1. dream	dream	dream	draem	dream
2. real	real	reat	real	real
3. speak	speak	speak	speak	speah
4. leap	laep	leap	leap	leap

C Fill in the boxes with the correct spelling words.

1.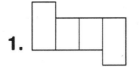

2.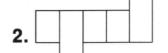

3.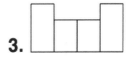

4.

5.

6.

© 2001 Steck-Vaughn Company. All Rights Reserved.

Name _____

Words with *ea*

real	beak	dream
deal	speak	leap

A Circle the word that is the same as the top one.

real	speak	dream	leap	deal	beak
reel	speah	drean	leab	lead	deak
rael	speak	dreaw	leep	deal	beah
neal	sgeak	dream	leap	beal	beek
real	spaek	bream	leeq	dcal	beak

B Answer each question with a spelling word.

1. Which word means "to jump"? _____

2. Which word means "a bird's mouth"? _____

3. Which word can mean "an agreement"? _____

4. Which word means "true"? _____

C Write each spelling word three times in cursive.

deal _____

dream _____

beak _____

leap _____

real _____

speak _____

Lesson 7

Words with *ai*

paid	mail	plain
wait	trail	brain

A Fill in each blank with a spelling word.

1. I am _____ a dollar a week for washing dishes.

2. We ride our bikes on the _____ through the park.

3. You think with your _____.

4. Today I received a letter in the _____.

5. Please _____ for me at the corner.

6. Do you like hamburgers _____ or with cheese?

B Fill in the boxes with the correct spelling words.

1.    2. 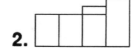   3.

C Circle the word that is the same as the top one.

mail	trail	plain	wait	paid	brain
maid	tnail	plaiu	wait	baig	bnain
mail	frail	blain	mait	qaid	brain
wail	train	plain	waif	paid	prain
mial	trail	plian	wiat	daid	braiu

Name _____

© 2001 Steck-Vaughn Company. All Rights Reserved.

DAY 2

Words with *ai*

paid	mail	plain
wait	trail	brain

A Write the spelling words in ABC order.

1. _____   2. _____   3. _____

4. _____   5. _____   6. _____

B Match each word with its picture. Then write the word.

1. wait   _____

2. mail   _____

3. trail   _____

4. brain   _____

5. paid   _____

C Use the correct spelling words to complete the story.

I was helping Mrs. Lee with her garage sale when I

noticed an old clock for sale. The clock wasn't fancy. It was very

_____. I liked it so much that I _____ ten dollars

for it. I could not _____ to look for more things to buy.

DAY
3

Words with *ai*

paid	mail	plain
wait	trail	brain

A Find the missing letters. Then write the word.

1. p ____ ____ ____ ____   _____

2. ____ ____ ____ ____ l   _____

3. ____ ____ ____ t   _____

B Write the spelling word that rhymes with the word pair.

1. stain   brain   _____

2. sail   trail   _____

3. maid   raid   _____

4. bait   trait   _____

C Find each hidden word from the list.

mail	wait	paid	plain
trail	bait	maid	brain
rail	trait	raid	grain
bail	gait	aid	train

```
b  m  a  i  l  o  r  r  a  i  d  v  w  t  n
r  a  i  l  t  m  g  r  i  b  a  i  t  r  o
a  i  b  c  e  p  a  i  d  v  w  x  r  a  n
i  d  w  a  i  t  i  a  n  l  q  b  a  i  l
n  g  r  a  i  n  t  r  a  i  n  t  i  t  r
c  l  b  p  l  a  i  n  j  w  c  v  l  x  d
```

Name _____

© 2001 Steck-Vaughn Company. All Rights Reserved.

31

Words with *ai*

paid	mail	plain
wait	trail	brain

A Answer each question with a spelling word.

1. Which word can mean "a path"? _____

2. Which word can mean "mind"? _____

3. Which word can mean "simple"? _____

B Circle the letters that are the same in each spelling word.

paid   mail   wait   trail   plain   brain

C Use each spelling word in a sentence.

1. plain _____

2. wait _____

3. paid _____

D Write each spelling word three times in cursive.

paid _____

plain _____

mail _____

wait _____

brain _____

trail _____

Lesson 8

Words with *oo*

broom	moon	tool
groom	spoon	cool

A Fill in each blank with a spelling word.

1. The _____ can be seen mostly at night.

2. A hammer is a _____ used by a carpenter.

3. The air feels _____ in the fall.

4. The bride and _____ were married today.

5. The larger _____ is for the soup.

6. We use a _____ to sweep the patio.

B Fill in the boxes with the correct spelling words.

1. 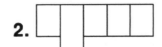   2.   3.

C Circle the word that is the same as the top one.

broom	groom	moon	spoon	tool	cool
broon	groom	noom	spoom	toot	aool
bromm	groam	moom	sgoon	tool	coot
broom	grume	moan	spoon	loot	cool
droom	groon	moon	spoou	toal	coal

© 2001 Steck-Vaughn Company. All Rights Reserved.

Name _____

Words with *oo*

broom	**moon**	**tool**
groom	**spoon**	**cool**

A Use the correct spelling words to complete the story.

Summer had come to an end, and I was looking forward to the time of the year when the leaves change colors. I waited and waited, and then one night I noticed something.

The air was _____, and the wind was crisp. The _____ above was full and round. I could hear something rustling on my front porch. I looked to see what it was. I couldn't believe my eyes! There were so many leaves on my porch. And they were the most beautiful colors. I needed to clear a path, so I took my _____ and began to sweep. After I finished, I made a cup of hot chocolate. It was so hot I had to sip my drink from a _____.

B Match each word with its picture. Then write the word.

1. broom

 _____

2. spoon

 _____

3. tool

 _____

Lesson 8 | Words with *oo*

DAY 3

broom	moon	tool
groom	spoon	cool

A Find the missing letters. Then write the word.

1. ____ p ____ ____ ____   _____

2. c ____ ____ ____   _____

3. b ____ ____ ____ ____   _____

B Find each hidden word from the list.

been	before	give	after	again	once
were	when	always	because	round	put
some	his	how	just	ask	thank

```
a  l  b  e  c  a  u  s  e  j  u  s  s  r  e  h
f  l  i  v  e  g  p  c  o  u  l  d  e  o  s  i
t  h  a  n  k  a  u  o  n  s  c  a  b  u  o  s
e  v  e  r  y  i  t  u  c  t  w  h  e  n  m  o
r  e  h  o  o  n  i  b  e  f  o  r  e  d  e  u
k  n  o  w  a  r  g  i  v  e  v  i  n  a  s  k
n  o  w  e  r  e  w  a  l  w  a  y  s  t  o  e
```

C Use each spelling word in a sentence.

1. moon _____

2. groom _____

3. cool _____

4. tool _____

© 2001 Steck-Vaughn Company. All Rights Reserved.

Name _____

Lesson 8

Words with *oo*

broom	moon	tool
groom	spoon	cool

A Answer each question with a spelling word.

1. Which word is something to sweep with? _____

2. Which word means "not very cold"? _____

3. Which word is something to eat with? _____

B Put an *X* on the word that is <u>not</u> the same.

1.	groom	groom	groom	qroom	groom
2.	tool	tool	fool	tool	tool
3.	moon	moon	moon	moon	moor

C Circle the letters that are the same in each spelling word.

broom   tool   spoon   groom   cool   moon

D Write each spelling word three times in cursive.

tool _____

broom _____

cool _____

groom _____

moon _____

spoon _____

36

Words with *oa*

boat	toast	load
throat	coast	road

A **Fill in each blank with a spelling word.**

1. I can _____ the box into the car.

2. I only like to have eggs and _____ for breakfast.

3. It's fun to _____ down a hill on a bike.

4. My _____ feels sore.

5. Have you ever sailed a _____?

6. This _____ goes west to Texas.

B **Circle the word that is the same as the top one.**

load	throat	toast	road	coast	boat
loed	thnoat	toast	raod	coost	boot
loab	throot	toost	roab	caost	boat
load	thoatt	taost	rood	cosat	doat
laod	throat	toats	road	coast	bote

C **Write the spelling words in ABC order.**

1. _____   2. _____   3. _____

4. _____   5. _____   6. _____

Name _____

© 2001 Steck-Vaughn Company. All Rights Reserved.

Words with *oa*

boat	toast	load
throat	coast	road

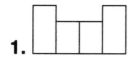 Write the spelling words that have the *oa* pattern.

_____   _____   _____

_____   _____   _____

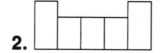 Fill in the boxes with the correct spelling words.

1.

2.

3.

4.

5.

6.

C Use each spelling word in a sentence.

1. load _____

2. toast _____

3. boat _____

4. coast _____

5. throat _____

6. road _____

DAY 3

Words with *oa*

boat	toast	load
throat	coast	road

A Write each correct spelling word beside its clue.

_____ **1.** This travels on water.

_____ **2.** It hurts to swallow when this is sore.

_____ **3.** This is also called a street.

_____ **4.** Land near the sea is called this.

_____ **5.** This is something heavy that you carry.

_____ **6.** You might have this for breakfast.

B Put an *X* on the word that is <u>not</u> the same.

1.	load	load	loab	load	load
2.	boat	boat	boat	boat	boaf
3.	toast	toast	toast	tosat	toast
4.	road	road	raob	road	road
5.	throat	throaf	throat	throat	throat

C Write a spelling word under each picture.

1. _____   **2.** _____   **3.** _____

Name _____

© 2001 Steck-Vaughn Company. All Rights Reserved.

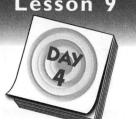

DAY 4

Words with *oa*

boat	toast	load
throat	coast	road

A Find the missing letters. Then write the word.

1. t ____ ____ ____ ____ t   _____

2. r ____ ____ ____   _____

B Use the correct spelling words to complete the story.

I am taking a trip to Florida in the summer. I'm looking forward to the sun and sand since I have never been to the _____ before. I will be meeting a friend there. She lives very close to the beach. She also has a _____ that she keeps at the marina. Maybe I will learn how to water-ski. I'd better start thinking about what I will pack. I always bring a heavy _____ when I travel.

C Write each spelling word three times in cursive.

boat _____

toast _____

load _____

throat _____

road _____

coast _____

Lesson 10   Words with *a*(consonant)*e*

blade	flake	scale
shade	snake	whale

A   **Fill in each blank with a spelling word.**

1. I saw a _____ when I was hiking in the woods.

2. A _____ of snow fell in my hand.

3. The _____ is the largest living mammal.

4. You can make a whistle with a _____ of grass.

5. Weigh the fruit on the _____.

6. I try to stand in the _____ when it's hot.

B   **Circle the word that is the same as the top one.**

blade	shade	flake	snake	scale	whale
blode	shabe	floke	smake	seale	vhale
dlade	shode	flabe	snake	scole	whole
blabe	shade	flake	snoke	scale	wbale
blade	slade	flakc	snabe	scalc	whale

C   **Find the missing letters. Then write the word.**

1. ____ c ____ ____ ____   _____

2. ____ h ____ d ____   _____

3. f l ____ ____ ____   _____

Name _____

41

© 2001 Steck-Vaughn Company. All Rights Reserved.

Lesson 10

Words with *a*(consonant)*e*

blade	flake	scale
shade	snake	whale

A Write the three pairs of spelling words that rhyme.

1. _____ _____

2. _____ _____

3. _____ _____

B Fill in the boxes with the correct spelling words.

1.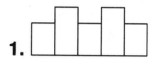

2.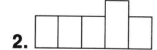

3.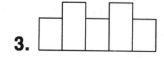

4.

5.

6.

C Write a spelling word under each picture.

1. _____ 2. _____ 3. _____

D Complete each sentence.

1. When I saw the <u>snake</u>, _____.

2. A <u>flake</u> of snow _____.

42

Lesson 10

Words with *a*(consonant)*e*

blade	flake	scale
shade	snake	whale

A Find each hidden word from the list.

shade	blade	tale	stale	rake	lake
jade	glade	sale	ale	flake	wake
wade	made	scale	gale	snake	bake
spade	grade	shale	pale	stake	cake

```
b  l  a  d  e  a  s  b  a  s  j  e  l  a  m  a
r  a  k  e  g  r  n  k  e  t  a  l  e  n  a  t
a  k  s  w  r  l  a  s  h  a  d  e  w  a  d  s
b  e  c  a  a  s  k  p  a  l  e  a  h  g  e  a
e  t  a  d  d  t  e  a  l  e  a  m  o  l  a  l
g  a  l  e  e  a  a  d  e  a  m  f  l  a  k  e
l  a  e  w  a  k  e  e  a  c  a  k  e  d  a  m
a  s  h  a  l  e  b  a  k  e  a  d  e  e  l  a
```

B Use the correct spelling words to complete the poem.

I stopped beside the garden on a bright spring day.

A _____ of grass, and then another,

Moved along the way.

I got down on my hands and knees,

A closer look to take.

And in a patch of _____ I saw

A tiny garter _____.

Name _____

© 2001 Steck-Vaughn Company. All Rights Reserved.

Lesson 10

Words with *a*(consonant)*e*

blade	flake	scale
shade	snake	whale

A Answer each question with a spelling word.

1. Which word is a large animal that lives in the sea?

   _____

2. Which word can mean "a plant leaf"? _____

3. Which word is part of a fish? _____

4. Which word is a piece of snow? _____

5. Which word means "an area without sun"? _____

B Write words that begin like each spelling word below.

   <u>wh</u>ale   <u>fl</u>ake   <u>sn</u>ake   <u>b</u>lade

   _____   _____   _____   _____

   _____   _____   _____   _____

C Write each spelling word three times in cursive.

blade _____

flake _____

whale _____

shade _____

scale _____

snake _____

Review

real	mail	spoon
deal	trail	moon
beak	plain	broom
speak	brain	groom
dream	leap	paid

A Write a spelling word under each picture.

1. _____ 2. _____ 3. _____

4. _____ 5. _____ 6. _____

B Fill in each blank with a spelling word.

1. She _____ six dollars for the ticket.

2. I swept the kitchen floor with a _____.

3. The bride and _____ were married today.

4. The parrot's _____ is very sharp.

5. Is the wrapping paper _____ or fancy?

6. I only use _____ butter on my toast.

7. My _____ is tired from so much thinking.

© 2001 Steck-Vaughn Company. All Rights Reserved.

Name _____

Review

tool	load	scale
cool	road	whale
boat	flake	blade
throat	snake	shade
toast	coast	wait

C **Write the spelling word that rhymes with the word pair.**

1. load   toad   _____

2. bake   snake   _____

3. made   blade   _____

4. boast   coast   _____

5. pool   cool   _____

6. bait   trait   _____

D **Use the correct spelling words to complete the story.**

Have you ever seen a real _____ out in the ocean?

They are huge! Once I traveled by_____ far out into the

waters of the Atlantic Ocean. We could not see land because

we were so far from the _____. We had to wait and

watch a while. Then we saw them! Great humpback whales were

swimming very close to our boat. They seemed to like to stay

together. But one swam under our boat! They were the most

amazing animals I had ever seen.

Lesson 11

Words with *a*(consonant)*e*

cane	scrape	base
pane	grape	case

A Fill in each blank with a spelling word.

1. We had to _____ the ice off the windshield.

2. Bring a hat in _____ it is cold.

3. A walking stick is called a _____.

4. The runner slid into third _____.

5. That window has one _____ of glass.

6. Do you like orange or _____ juice?

B Fill in the boxes with the correct spelling words.

1.

2.

3.

4.

5.

6.

C Find the missing letters. Then write the word.

1. c ____ s ____   _____

2. ____ ____ ____ p ____   _____

3. p ____ ____ ____   _____

© 2001 Steck-Vaughn Company. All Rights Reserved.

Name _____

DAY 2

Words with *a*(consonant)*e*

cane	scrape	base
pane	grape	case

A Circle the word that is the same as the top one.

grape	base	pane	scrape	case	cane
grope	bose	pame	scrage	cose	came
grage	base	panc	scrape	casc	canc
grape	dase	paen	sceape	case	cone
grapc	baes	pane	serape	ease	cane

B Put an *X* on the word that is <u>not</u> the same.

1. scrape	scrape	scrape	scarpe	scrape
2. grape	grape	grape	grape	gnape
3. pane	pane	pane	pane	pare

C Use each spelling word in a sentence.

1. cane _____

2. pane _____

3. scrape _____

4. grape _____

5. base _____

6. case _____

Lesson 11

Words with *a*(consonant)*e*

DAY 3

cane	scrape	base
pane	grape	case

A Write a spelling word under each picture.

1. _____   2. _____   3. _____

4. _____   5. _____   6. _____

B Write the spelling words in ABC order.

1. _____   2. _____   3. _____

4. _____   5. _____   6. _____

C Answer each question with a spelling word.

1. Which word means "a stem" or "a stick"? _____

2. Which word names a fruit? _____

3. Which word can mean "the bottom of"? _____

4. Which word means "to rub hard"? _____

5. Which word sounds the same as "pain"? _____

6. Which word rhymes with "base"? _____

© 2001 Steck-Vaughn Company. All Rights Reserved.

Name _____

Words with *a*(consonant)*e*

cane	scrape	base
pane	grape	case

A Put an *X* on the word that is <u>not</u> the same.

1. scrape	scrape	scrape	scarpe	scrape
2. pane	pane	pane	pane	pare
3. case	case	caes	case	case
4. grape	grape	grape	grage	grape
5. cane	came	cane	cane	cane

B Write the spelling word that rhymes with the word pair.

1. vase   case   _____

2. tape   scrape   _____

3. lane   cane   _____

C Use the correct spelling words to complete the story.

Every weekend my friend and I go to the creek. It's close to my house, at the _____ of a hill.

My friend always brings a bucket, in _____ we catch some fish. I always bring _____ juice for us to drink.

Tomorrow I'm supposed to bring the bait. I think I'll take some leftover pizza. If the fish don't want to eat it, then I will.

Lesson 12 Words with *a*(consonant)*e*

plate	tame	pave
state	flame	brave

A Fill in each blank with a spelling word.

1. I had to be _____ to climb the tree.

2. What _____ do you live in?

3. The fire burned with a hot _____.

4. They are going to _____ the road in front of our house.

5. I put pizza and salad on my _____.

6. The zoo has both wild and _____ animals.

B Circle the word that is the same as the top one.

plate	flame	brave	state	tame	pave
platc	ftame	brove	state	tane	pove
plote	flame	drave	slate	tame	pawe
ptale	flane	brave	stote	tome	pave
plate	flome	braue	stale	tamc	pavc

C Find the missing letters. Then write the word.

1. p ____ ____ ____   _____

2. ____ t ____ ____ ____   _____

3. ____ ____ ____ m ____   _____

4. ____ r ____ ____ ____   _____

Name _____

© 2001 Steck-Vaughn Company. All Rights Reserved.

Words with *a*(consonant)*e*

plate	tame	pave
state	flame	brave

A Fill in the boxes with the correct spelling words.

1.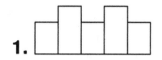

2.

3.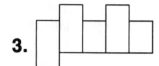

4.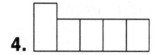

5.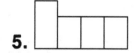

6.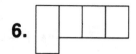

B Write a spelling word under each picture.

1. _____   2. _____   3. _____

C Fill in each blank with a spelling word.

1. Alaska is the largest one. _____

2. This is the opposite of "afraid" or "fearful." _____

3. What appears when you light a candle? _____

4. What do you do to make a rough road smooth? _____

5. This word is the opposite of "wild." _____

6. This word is a kind of dish. _____

Words with *a*(consonant)*e*

plate	tame	pave
state	flame	brave

A) Write the spelling words in ABC order.

1. _____ 2. _____ 3. _____

4. _____ 5. _____ 6. _____

B) Write the spelling word that rhymes with the word pair.

1. same   flame   _____

2. save   pave   _____

3. plate   date   _____

C) Write the four spelling words that begin with a consonant blend (two letters that make one sound).

_____   _____

_____   _____

D) Use each spelling word in a sentence.

1. plate _____

2. state _____

3. tame _____

4. flame _____

Name _____

© 2001 Steck-Vaughn Company. All Rights Reserved.

Words with *a*(consonant)*e*

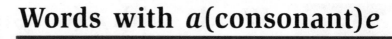

DAY 4

plate	tame	pave
state	flame	brave

A **Make new words. Drop the *e*. Then add *ing*.**

1. tame + ing = <u>taming</u>   2. state + ing = _____

3. pave + ing = _____   4. flame + ing = _____

B **Write each spelling word three times in cursive.**

brave _____

plate _____

tame _____

state _____

flame _____

C **Use the correct spelling words to complete the story.**

Last Saturday night we saw a special TV show. It was

about a three-ring circus. The circus traveled from state to

_____.

There was a very _____ man who worked with

lions. He had the lions jump through a hoop that had a

_____.

I **would never** want to stand too close to a lion, even if the lion

was _____.

Words with *i*(consonant)*e*

glide	life	bike
pride	wife	strike

A Fill in each blank with a spelling word.

1. His _____ teaches math at the high school.

2. My paper airplanes _____ through the air.

3. Her _____ is a ten-speed.

4. She takes great _____ in her work.

5. A butterfly's _____ span is very short.

6. Did lightning _____ that tree?

B Circle the word that is the same as the top one.

glide	wife	bike	pride	life	strike
glidc	vife	biek	pribe	lufe	stnike
glibe	wifc	bike	pride	lile	strile
gliae	wife	bikc	pnide	lifc	strike
glide	wief	bile	pridc	life	strikc

C Find the missing letters. Then write the word.

1. ____ l ____ ____ ____   _____

2. w ____ ____ ____   _____

3. p ____ ____ d ____   _____

© 2001 Steck-Vaughn Company. All Rights Reserved.

Name _____

Words with *i*(consonant)*e*

glide	life	bike
pride	wife	strike

A Fill in the boxes with the correct spelling words.

1.

2.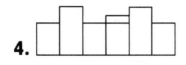

3.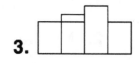

4.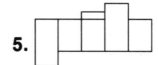

5.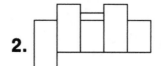

6.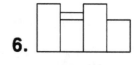

B Write the spelling words in ABC order.

1. _____   2. _____   3. _____

4. _____   5. _____   6. _____

C Answer each question with a spelling word.

1. Which word means "to hit something" or "to make a good score in bowling"? _____

2. Which word belongs with "husband"? _____

3. Which word means "a good feeling about yourself"?

_____

4. Which word is short for "bicycle"? _____

5. Which word rhymes with "wife"? _____

DAY 3

Words with *i*(consonant)*e*

glide	life	bike
pride	wife	strike

A Use each spelling word in a sentence.

1. pride _____

2. bike _____

3. life _____

B Write words that begin like each spelling word below.

<u>g</u>lide   <u>pr</u>ide   <u>w</u>ife   <u>str</u>ike

_____   _____   _____   _____

_____   _____   _____   _____

C Make new words. Drop the *e*. Then add *ing*.

1. glide + ing = _____   2. bike + ing = _____

3. strike + ing = _____   4. pride + ing = _____

D Put an *X* on the word that is <u>not</u> the same.

1.	wife	wile	wife	wife	wife
2.	pride	pride	pride	pride	pnide
3.	bike	bike	bike	bika	bike
4.	glide	glide	qlide	glide	glide

© 2001 Steck-Vaughn Company. All Rights Reserved.

Name _____

Lesson 13

Words with *i*(consonant)*e*

DAY 4

glide	life	bike
pride	wife	strike

A Write each spelling word three times in cursive.

glide

pride

life

wife

strike

bike

B Write the spelling word that rhymes with the word pair.

1. like   bike   _____

2. slide   glide   _____

C Use the correct spelling words to complete the poem.

On a fine spring day

When _____ is great,

And all my work is over,

I love to ride,

To pedal and _____,

On my _____ through fields of clover.

Words with *i*(consonant)*e*

mile	dime	vine
while	grime	spine

A Fill in each blank with a spelling word.

1. I will write to you _____ I am away.

2. Your _____ is in the middle of your back.

3. I hope the ivy _____ will grow.

4. She runs a _____ every day.

5. The car engine was covered with _____.

6. This piece of bubble gum cost me a _____.

B Find the missing letters. Then write the word.

1. ____ ____ ____ l ____   _____

2. ____ ____ ____ n ____   _____

3. ____ ____ m ____   _____

C Answer each question with a spelling word.

1. Which word names a certain distance? _____

2. Which word is the same as two nickels? _____

3. Which word names a part of the body? _____

4. Which word names a kind of plant? _____

5. Which word can mean the same as "dirt"? _____

© 2001 Steck-Vaughn Company. All Rights Reserved.

Name _____

Words with *i*(consonant)*e*

mile	dime	vine
while	grime	spine

A Write the spelling words in ABC order.

1. _____ 2. _____ 3. _____

4. _____ 5. _____ 6. _____

B Write the three pairs of spelling words that rhyme.

1. _____ _____

2. _____ _____

3. _____ _____

C Circle the word that is the same as the top one.

mile	dime	grime	vine	spine	while
milc	dine	gnime	wime	spime	whilc
mite	dimc	grine	vime	spine	wkich
nile	dime	grime	vinc	spnie	while
mile	dima	qrime	vine	sqine	wkile

D Complete each sentence.

1. Sit down while _____.

2. The vine was growing _____.

60

Words with *i*(consonant)*e*

mile	dime	vine
while	grime	spine

A Fill in the boxes with the correct spelling words.

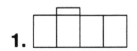

1.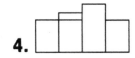

2.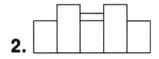

3.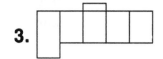

4.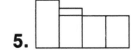

5.

6.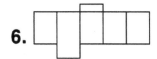

B Use the correct spelling words to complete the story.

We rode the roller coaster at the carnival. It gave me chills

all up and down my _____. I was so scared

_____ we sat at the top of the ride! When I looked

down, the ground seemed a _____ away.

C Use each spelling word in a sentence.

1. while _____

2. grime _____

3. spine _____

4. vine _____

5. dime _____

© 2001 Steck-Vaughn Company. All Rights Reserved.

Name _____

Words with *i*(consonant)*e*

mile	dime	vine
while	grime	spine

A Find each hidden word from the list.

grime	slime	nine	file	tile	vine
mime	crime	fine	rile	spine	rime
prime	line	mile	pile	twine	lime
time	mine				

```
t   i   l   e   t   o   l   d   p   i   e
o   t   h   e   s   e   i   t   r   s   o
p   i   l   e   l   i   n   t   i   m   e
c   a   t   w   i   n   e   o   m   i   s
r   g   r   i   m   i   t   v   e   l   p
i   r   i   l   e   n   f   i   l   e   i
m   i   m   e   w   e   i   n   i   t   n
e   m   e   o   m   i   n   e   m   o   e
t   e   e   s   h   i   e   c   e   s   s
```

B Write each spelling word three times in cursive.

mile

while

dime

vine

grime

spine

Lesson 15 Words with *i*(consonant)*e*

ripe	wise	drive
stripe	bite	why

A Fill in each blank with a spelling word.

1. _____ do you want to leave?

2. Skunks have a white _____ on their back.

3. I want to learn to _____ a car.

4. I had a _____ of the apple.

5. We will pick the fruit when it is _____.

6. It is _____ to study hard.

B Circle the word that is the same as the top one.

why	ripe	stripe	wise	bite	drive
whg	nipe	stirpe	wise	bite	driwe
wky	rige	stnipe	wisc	dite	dnive
vhy	ripe	stripc	vise	bile	drive
why	ripc	stripe	wsie	bitc	brive

C Write the spelling words that rhyme with the words below.

       shy   five   fight

1. _____ 2. _____ 3. _____

© 2001 Steck-Vaughn Company. All Rights Reserved.

Name _____

Words with *i*(consonant)*e*

ripe	wise	drive
stripe	bite	why

A Fill in the boxes with the correct spelling words.

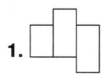

1.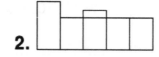

2.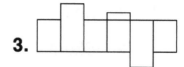

3.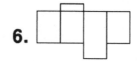

4.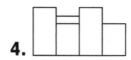

5.

6.

B Find the missing letters. Then write the word.

1. w ____ ____ ____   _____

2. ____ ____ ____ ____ e   _____

3. ____ ____ p ____   _____

C Answer each question with a spelling word.

1. Which word is used to ask a question? _____

2. Which word does "wisdom" come from? _____

3. Which word means "a long, narrow line"? _____

4. Which word can mean what you do with your teeth? _____

5. Which word means "to steer a car"? _____

6. Which word can mean "ready to eat"? _____

Words with *i*(consonant)*e*

ripe	wise	drive
stripe	bite	why

A Use the correct spelling words to complete the story.

The man who lives down the street is very _____.

He visits with his neighbors and friends every day, and he

always offers great advice.

He never learned to _____ a car. Instead, he walks

everywhere he needs to go. I asked him if he would ever like

to learn to drive. "_____ should I drive, when I can

exercise?" he said. He sure is wise!

B Use each spelling word in a sentence.

1. why _____

2. bite _____

3. stripe _____

4. ripe _____

C Write a spelling word under each picture.

1. _____   2. _____   3. _____

© 2001 Steck-Vaughn Company. All Rights Reserved.

Name _____

Words with *i*(consonant)*e*

ripe	wise	drive
stripe	bite	why

A Write each spelling word three times in cursive.

ripe

bite

stripe

wise

why

drive

B Find each hidden word from the list.

pipe	ripe	bite	dive	wise
stripe	wipe	white	five	
swipe	write	hive	why	

```
o  p  s  o  b  r  i  n  g  p  r  e  a  c  h  a
j  a  w  h  i  t  e  e  h  i  v  e  x  a  f  l
o  p  i  o  t  e  a  t  o  p  t  i  o  n  i  n
l  o  p  e  e  w  w  i  s  e  c  t  s  s  v  o
a  t  e  v  e  n  r  x  e  a  f  r  i  t  e  d
l  i  v  e  s  n  i  p  e  a  r  i  p  r  y  e
o  x  e  n  i  t  t  r  y  w  i  p  e  i  o  x
a  d  d  o  t  e  e  p  k  h  e  e  e  p  u  t
d  r  i  p  e  a  t  o  i  y  d  i  v  e  v  e
l  a  e  m  a  k  l  e  a  c  a  k  e  d  a  m
```

Review

cane	plate	pave
pane	state	brave
scrape	tame	glide
grape	flame	pride
base	case	drive

A Write a spelling word under each picture.

1. _____ 2. _____ 3. _____

4. _____ 5. _____ 6. _____

B Fill in each blank with a spelling word.

1. She slid into home _____.

2. Soon they will _____ the rough road.

3. The petting zoo has animals that are _____.

4. We had to _____ the ice off the windshield.

5. She takes great _____ in her work.

6. He was very _____ to climb the steep mountain.

7. My cousin is learning how to _____ a car.

© 2001 Steck-Vaughn Company. All Rights Reserved.

Name _____

Review

life	mile	vine
wife	while	spine
bike	dime	ripe
strike	grime	stripe
bite	wise	why

C Write the spelling word that rhymes with the word pair.

1. ripe   gripe   _____

2. bike   like   _____

3. time   dime   _____

4. knife   life   _____

5. site   white   _____

6. by   my   _____

D Use the correct spelling words to complete the poem.

Have you ever walked a _____

With a stone in your shoe all the _____?

It's enough to make your _____ tingle

And any _____ in your pocket jingle.

A _____ person will remove that stone

To help make _____ have a better tone.

Words with *o*(consonant)*e*

code	joke	home
rode	broke	know

A Fill in each blank with a spelling word.

1. The note is written in _____.

2. I _____ the bus downtown.

3. I must be _____ by dark.

4. The baseball hit the window and _____ it.

5. Please tell me a funny _____.

6. Do you _____ if snakes lay eggs?

B Circle the word that is the same as the top one.

home	broke	joke	code	know	rode
hame	brake	jokc	coed	knom	node
hone	broke	johe	cade	krow	rode
homc	brokc	jake	code	know	robe
home	bnoke	joke	eodc	hnow	rabe

C Find the missing letters. Then write the word.

1. ____ r ____ ____ ____   _____

2. ____ ____ m ____   _____

3. ____ ____ o ____   _____

© 2001 Steck-Vaughn Company. All Rights Reserved.

Name _____

Words with *o*(consonant)*e*

code	joke	home
rode	broke	know

A Fill in the boxes with the correct spelling words.

1.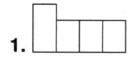

2.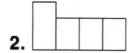

3.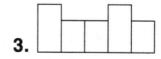

4.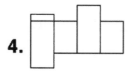

5.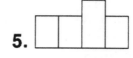

6.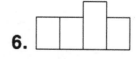

B Use each spelling word in a sentence.

1. know _____

2. home _____

3. rode _____

4. broke _____

5. code _____

6. joke _____

C Write the spelling word that rhymes with the word pair.

1. row   flow   _____

2. mode   rode   _____

3. smoke   joke   _____

Words with *o*(consonant)*e*

code	joke	home
rode	broke	know

A Write the spelling words in ABC order.

1. _____ 2. _____ 3. _____

4. _____ 5. _____ 6. _____

B Put an *X* on the word that is <u>not</u> the same.

1. code	code	cobe	code	code
2. know	know	know	know	knom
3. rode	rode	node	rode	rode
4. broke	broke	broke	brohe	broke
5. home	hone	home	home	home
6. joke	joke	joke	joke	jake

C Use the correct spelling words to complete the story.

Yesterday I bought a new bike from the store. I was so

excited about my bike that I _____ it for two miles. I

was on my way _____ when all of a sudden, I felt

something pop. My bicycle chain was broken. This was not

funny! This was not a _____! Now I _____

I should look closer at things before I buy them.

Name _____

© 2001 Steck-Vaughn Company. All Rights Reserved.

Words with *o*(consonant)*e*

code	joke	home
rode	broke	know

A Write each spelling word three times in cursive.

broke

home

know

rode

joke

B Figure out what the message in code says.

1	2	3	4	5	6	7	8	9	10	11	12	13
A	B	C	D	E	F	G	H	I	J	K	L	M

14	15	16	17	18	19	20	21	22	23	24	25	26
N	O	P	Q	R	S	T	U	V	W	X	Y	Z

13 1 25   20 8 5   6 15 18 3 5   2 5

23 9 20 8   25 15 21   15 14   25 15 21 18

19 16 5 12 12 9 14 7   20 5 19 20 .

Lesson 17 — Words with *o*(consonant)*e*

pole	slope	note
stone	rose	drove

A Fill in each blank with a spelling word.

1. The sun _____ at 6:30 this morning.

2. She used a _____ for fishing.

3. He wrote a _____ to his friend.

4. She will ski down the _____ this afternoon.

5. I _____ my grandmother to the bus station.

6. The path is made of _____.

B Circle the vowels that are in the spelling words.

a e i o u

Put an *X* on the vowel that is silent.

a e i o u

C Circle the word that is the same as the top one.

pole	stone	slope	rose	note	drove
polc	sfone	slope	ruse	rote	brove
qole	stone	slopc	rosc	note	droue
gole	store	sloge	rose	nofe	dnove
pole	stonc	slode	nose	notc	drove

Name _____

73

© 2001 Steck-Vaughn Company. All Rights Reserved.

Lesson 17

DAY 2

Words with *o*(consonant)*e*

pole	slope	note
stone	rose	drove

A Use the correct spelling words to answer these riddles.

1. This can mean "went up." It is also a flower.

   What is it? _____

2. It may look like this— or like this—

   What is it? _____

3. It goes up or down at an angle. It can look like

   this—

   What is it? _____

B Write the spelling word that rhymes with the word pair.

1. hole   mole   _____

2. wove   grove   _____

3. tone   bone   _____

C Fill in the boxes with the correct spelling words.

1. 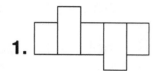   2. 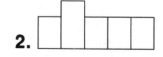   3.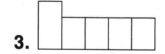

74

DAY 3

Words with *o*(consonant)*e*

pole	slope	note
stone	rose	drove

A Find the missing letters. Then write the word.

1. ____ ____ ____ p ____   _____

2. ____ r ____ ____ ____   _____

B Use the correct spelling words to complete the story.

When the moon _____ last night, it was full. I went

outside in the yard. There was plenty of light. Our _____

wall made a long shadow on the lawn. All was still, until a car

_____ by and some dogs started barking. I was so

scared, but I knew I was just being silly.

C Write a spelling word under each picture.

          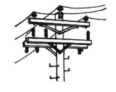

1. _____   2. _____   3. _____

D Complete each sentence.

1. The <u>stone</u> path _____.

2. I found a <u>note</u> that _____.

Name _____

© 2001 Steck-Vaughn Company. All Rights Reserved.

Lesson 17 — Words with *o*(consonant)*e*

pole	slope	note
stone	rose	drove

A Write the spelling words in ABC order.

1. _____   2. _____   3. _____

4. _____   5. _____   6. _____

B Use spelling words to complete the puzzle.

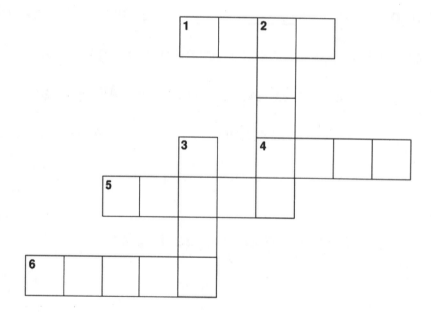

ACROSS

1. a flower

4. something written down

5. an angle or a slant

6. My sister _____ the car to the store.

DOWN

2. a rock

3. a long stick

76

Lesson 18

Words with *-old* and *-ow*

hold	snow	own
cold	throw	don't

A Fill in each blank with a spelling word.

1. How far can you _____ the softball?

2. Wear your coat if it's _____ outside.

3. We _____ have school today.

4. He has his _____ book.

5. The rain will soon turn to _____.

6. She will _____ the door open for us.

B Circle the word that is the same as the top one.

snow	throw	don't	cold	own	hold
srow	thnow	don't	colb	owr	holb
snom	throm	don'f	colp	own	kold
snow	fhrow	bon't	cold	omn	hald
snaw	throw	dor't	cald	awn	hold

C Write the spelling word that rhymes with the word pair.

1. fold   hold   _____

2. snow   slow   _____

3. blown   grown   _____

Name _____

77

© 2001 Steck-Vaughn Company. All Rights Reserved.

DAY
2

Words with *-old* and *-ow*

hold	snow	own
cold	throw	don't

A Write the spelling words in ABC order.

1. _____ 2. _____ 3. _____

4. _____ 5. _____ 6. _____

B Find the missing letters. Then write the word.

1. ____ ____ ____ o ____   _____

2. h ____ ____ d   _____

3. c ____ ____ ____   _____

C Use the correct spelling words to complete the story.

Last night a winter storm brought _____ to our

town. When I woke up, our whole yard was covered. I went

outside to take a walk. I _____ know if I've ever been

as _____ as I was today.

D Write a spelling word under each picture.

1. _____   2. _____   3. _____

DAY 3

Words with *-old* and *-ow*

hold	snow	own
cold	throw	don't

A Use each spelling word in a cursive sentence.

snow   The snow is cold.

don't

hold

throw

cold

own

B Fill in the boxes with the correct spelling words.

1.

2.

3.

4.

5.

6.

C Write the spelling word that matches its antonym (opposite).

1. do _____

2. catch _____

3. hot _____

Name _____

© 2001 Steck-Vaughn Company. All Rights Reserved.

Words with -old and -ow

hold	snow	own
cold	throw	don't

A Complete each sentence.

1. We <u>own</u> _____.

2. <u>Hold</u> this _____.

3. He can <u>throw</u> _____.

B Find each hidden word from the list.

cold	fold	bow	tow	snow	throw
hold	gold	low	glow	stow	blown
bold	sold	mow	blow	grow	own
old	told	row	flow	crow	grown
mold	scold	sow	slow	show	thrown

```
g  r  o  e  p  c  o  b  o  t  o  l  d
s  c  o  l  d  r  o  b  f  o  w  o  r
o  t  w  o  w  o  g  l  o  w  t  r  l
o  o  n  m  o  w  r  o  l  o  l  d  o
p  w  o  o  f  l  o  w  d  b  o  t  w
o  b  l  w  s  a  w  n  o  l  o  h  o
s  o  l  d  l  u  b  o  r  o  w  r  h
h  l  o  s  o  g  o  l  d  w  o  o  s
o  d  r  n  w  h  w  i  o  c  o  w  t
w  o  m  o  l  d  a  g  r  o  w  n  o
o  s  o  w  h  r  l  h  o  l  d  o  w
t  h  r  o  w  o  d  t  r  d  o  j  h
```

Words with -*air* and -*are*

fair	care	share
chair	spare	stare

A Fill in each blank with a spelling word.

1. I have a _____ tire in the trunk of my car.

2. We are going to a county _____.

3. The _____ is made of wood.

4. To look at something for a long time, means to _____.

5. She said she would _____ her dessert with me.

6. I will take _____ of my neighbor's cat.

B Write the spelling words in ABC order.

1. _____ 2. _____ 3. _____

4. _____ 5. _____ 6. _____

C Put an *X* on the word that is **not** the same.

1.	chair	chair	chair	chain	chair
2.	fair	fair	fair	fair	tair
3.	share	share	shore	share	share
4.	stare	stare	stare	sfare	stare
5.	care	care	core	care	care
6.	spare	spare	spare	spare	spaer

© 2001 Steck-Vaughn Company. All Rights Reserved.

Name _____

Words with *-air* and *-are*

fair	care	share
chair	spare	stare

A Circle the letters that are the same in each spelling word.

stare   share   spare   care

B Write the spelling word that fits both meanings.

_____   **1.** "to save" or "an extra tire"

_____   **2.** "to be in charge of a group" or "a seat"

_____   **3.** "equal and just" or "clear and sunny"

C Fill in the boxes with the correct spelling words.

1. 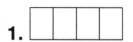   2. 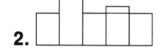   3.

4. 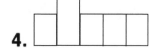   5.   6.

D Complete each sentence.

1. I <u>care</u> about _____.

2. He will <u>share</u> _____.

3. My <u>spare</u> tire _____.

4. The old <u>chair</u> _____.

DAY 3

Words with -*air* and -*are*

fair	care	share
chair	spare	stare

A Use each spelling word in a cursive sentence.

fair _____

chair _____

care _____

spare _____

share _____

stare _____

B Find the missing letters. Then write the word.

1. c ____ ____ ____   _____

2. c ____ ____ ____ ____   _____

3. ____ t a ____ ____   _____

C Write each correct spelling word beside its clue.

_____   1.   This is a seat. It belongs with a table.

_____   2.   To look at something for a long time.

_____   3.   If you're being equal and just,
              you're being this.

_____   4.   This can mean "to save."

© 2001 Steck-Vaughn Company. All Rights Reserved.

Name _____

Lesson 19

Words with -*air* and -*are*

fair	care	share
chair	spare	stare

A Complete each sentence with a spelling word.

1. "Fare" is a homonym (sounds the same) for _____.

2. The word that can mean "a seat" is _____.

3. The word that can mean "extra" is _____.

B Circle the word that is the same as the top one.

fair	chair	care	spare	share	stare
fare	chiar	cane	sqare	slare	stane
fain	chain	cana	spaer	shaer	stare
foir	ckain	cone	spare	shore	staer
fair	chair	care	apare	share	strae

C Use the correct spelling words to complete the story.

I have watched butterflies for two years. I know the names

of many kinds. When friends ask me questions about

butterflies, I can _____ the answers with them.

If you catch a butterfly, you must hold it with great

_____. Its wings are thin and can tear easily. It's

not _____ to keep them, so quickly let them go.

84

Words with *ar*

far	dark	art
scar	shark	start

A Fill in each blank with a spelling word.

1. The deep cut on his arm left a big _____.

2. The car would not _____ on cold mornings.

3. The _____ swam around in the tank.

4. In the summer, it gets _____ at 8:00 P.M.

5. How _____ do you live from here?

6. Did you paint in _____ class today?

B Fill in the boxes with the correct spelling words.

1.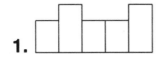

2.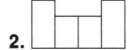

3.

4.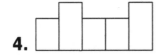

5.

6.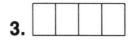

C Find the missing letters. Then write the word.

1. ____ ____ ____ ____ t   _____

2. ____ ____ ____ ____ k   _____

3. ____ ____ r   _____

Name _____

© 2001 Steck-Vaughn Company. All Rights Reserved.

Words with *ar*

far	dark	art
scar	shark	start

A Circle the word that is the same as the top one.

shark	art	far	start	scar	dark
shark	art	fan	stant	scan	bark
shank	arf	tar	start	sear	darh
skark	ant	fur	starf	scar	dark
sharh	anf	far	sfarf	soar	dank

B Write the spelling words in ABC order.

1. _____ 2. _____ 3. _____

4. _____ 5. _____ 6. _____

C Write each correct spelling word beside its clue.

_____ 1. This mark can stay on your skin after you have had a bad cut.

_____ 2. This word means "without light."

_____ 3. This word means "a long way" or "distant."

_____ 4. This animal lives in the ocean.

_____ 5. Drawing and painting are examples of this.

DAY 3

Words with *ar*

far	dark	art
scar	shark	start

A Put an *X* on the word that is <u>not</u> the same.

1. scar	scar	scan	scar	scar
2. shark	shark	shark	shrak	shark
3. start	start	slart	start	start

B Use each spelling word in a cursive sentence.

scar _____

start _____

dark _____

far _____

C Use the correct spelling words to complete the story.

I saw a strange painting at an _____ show. It

had light and _____ colors. The painting showed

plants and animals in the sea.

The largest animal was a _____. It had huge fins

and big round eyes. The shark was _____ below the

water's surface. The sea looked like a hidden world.

Name _____

© 2001 Steck-Vaughn Company. All Rights Reserved.

Words with *ar*

far	dark	art
scar	shark	start

A Write a spelling word under each picture.

1. _____   2. _____   3. _____

B Find each hidden word from the list.

far	par	ark	park	spar	dart
car	tar	bark	art	star	part
ajar	dark	spark	cart	start	jar
char	hark	stark	tart	chart	scar
lark	shark	mark			

```
b  c  s  c  a  r  d  f  g  h  b  a  t  j
k  l  p  m  n  p  f  u  l  l  a  q  r  t
s  t  a  r  t  s  a  t  c  a  r  v  w  a
t  x  r  y  a  z  r  b  h  c  k  p  a  r
a  r  k  d  r  f  g  m  a  h  j  k  l  t
r  m  n  p  q  s  h  a  r  k  r  s  d  t
k  v  h  u  r  t  w  r  x  y  z  b  a  c
d  f  a  g  h  a  j  k  k  s  p  a  r  l
p  a  r  t  l  r  m  n  p  q  a  s  t  r
v  j  k  x  a  y  z  c  h  a  r  t  b  c
d  a  r  k  r  d  m  a  r  f  k  g  j  h
j  r  l  m  k  n  p  r  q  s  l  v  a  w
a  r  t  x  h  a  r  t  y  z  g  a  r  b
```

Review

code	pole	don't
rode	stone	own
joke	slope	snow
broke	rose	throw
home	note	know

A Write a spelling word under each picture.

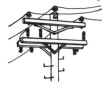 

1. _____ 2. _____ 3. _____

4. _____ 5. _____ 6. _____

B Fill in each blank with a spelling word.

1. She told her brother a funny _____.

2. I _____ know where you live.

3. The path leading to the lake is made of _____.

4. My aunt used to _____ three bicycles.

5. Do you _____ when the movie starts?

6. The glass pitcher fell to the ground and _____.

7. I will be _____ after six o'clock.

© 2001 Steck-Vaughn Company. All Rights Reserved.

Name _____

Review

drove	care	far
cold	spare	scar
hold	fair	dark
art	chair	shark
start	share	stare

C **Write the spelling word that rhymes with the word pair.**

1. star   far   _____

2. cold   fold   _____

3. dark   spark   _____

4. park   shark   _____

5. smart   start   _____

D **Use the correct spelling words to complete the story.**

I wanted to visit my grandfather who lives _____ away in another state. It was winter and quite _____. I wasn't sure if my car would _____, but it did. I _____ my car north to his house. By the time I arrived, it was nighttime.

Inside my grandfather's home, it was warm and toasty. He had built a fire. We each pulled up a _____ by the fire, and I listened to him tell stories about when he was a child.

Words with *-ear, -eer,* and *-row*

hear	**deer**	**arrow**
clear	**steer**	**narrow**

A Fill in each blank with a spelling word.

1. We climbed the steep, _____ path to the tower.

2. She will _____ out the boxes in the attic.

3. The big pine tree stood as straight as an _____.

4. Did you _____ the news today?

5. My family saw three _____ at the state park.

6. Is it hard to _____ a car?

B Find the missing letters. Then write the word.

1. ____ ____ r ____ ____   _____

2. ____ l ____ ____ ____   _____

3. ____ ____ e ____   _____

C Fill in the boxes with the correct spelling words.

1.

2.

3.

4.

5.

6.

© 2001 Steck-Vaughn Company. All Rights Reserved.

Name _____

Words with -*ear*, -*eer*, and -*row*

hear	deer	arrow
clear	steer	narrow

A Fill in each blank with the correct spelling word.

1. Write the words that have a silent *w*.

   _____ _____

2. Write the word that begins with *st*. _____

B Circle the word that is the same as the top one.

narrow	arrow	steer	clear	hear	deer
narrom	arnow	steen	clear	kear	dear
rarrow	arrow	sfeer	clean	hear	been
narrow	annow	stccr	cleer	near	peer
narruw	arrom	steer	elear	hean	deer

C Use the correct spelling words to complete the story.

A _____ was following a trail that was old and

_____. Far away, she could _____ the sound

of people hiking up the mountain. She tried to _____

away from them. She found a place to eat. The tender grass

was good. The deer lifted her head often to sniff the air and

listen for the hikers.

DAY 3

Words with *-ear, -eer,* and *-row*

hear	deer	arrow
clear	steer	narrow

A Use each spelling word in a cursive sentence.

arrow

narrow

hear

clear

deer

steer

B Write the spelling words in ABC order.

1. _____ 2. _____ 3. _____

4. _____ 5. _____ 6. _____

C Write each correct spelling word beside its clue.

_____ **1.** This belongs with a bow.

_____ **2.** This is a word for an animal and for what you do when you drive.

_____ **3.** The opposite of this word is "wide."

_____ **4.** You do this with your ears.

© 2001 Steck-Vaughn Company. All Rights Reserved.

Name _____

Words with *-ear, -eer,* and *-row*

hear	deer	arrow
clear	steer	narrow

A Write the spelling words that have a silent letter.

1. _____ 2. _____ 3. _____

4. _____ 5. _____ 6. _____

B Find each hidden word from the list.

veer	seer	ear	near	spear	farrow
deer	cheer	dear	rear	shear	harrow
jeer	steer	fear	sear	year	marrow
leer	sheer	gear	tear	arrow	narrow
peer	sneer	hear	clear	barrow	sparrow

```
b  c  s  d  s  t  e  e  r  f  h  x  g  h
c  j  n  k  e  l  m  n  p  f  e  a  r  q
l  e  e  r  a  r  s  t  v  a  a  r  w  x
e  y  e  z  r  s  h  e  e  r  r  r  b  g
a  b  r  c  d  f  g  a  h  r  j  o  k  e
r  l  m  n  s  p  a  r  r  o  w  w  p  a
v  e  a  r  q  e  d  r  s  w  v  e  e  r
t  v  w  x  d  e  e  r  k  i  n  d  l  y
s  h  e  a  r  r  a  z  b  a  r  r  o  w
b  a  c  d  e  f  r  g  h  n  j  s  n  j
k  r  l  n  a  r  r  o  w  e  m  p  g  e
n  r  v  a  r  p  q  r  s  a  t  e  v  e
w  o  s  e  e  r  y  e  a  r  x  a  y  r
z  w  b  c  h  e  e  r  m  a  r  r  o  w
```

Lesson 22

Words with *or*

world	bore	born
worth	snore	worn

A **Fill in each blank with a spelling word.**

1. Use a drill to _____ holes in the wood.

2. His pants were _____ at the knees.

3. Do you _____ when you sleep?

4. The new calf was _____ last night.

5. Why in the _____ did they do that?

6. How much do you think that car is _____?

B **Write the spelling words in ABC order.**

1. _____   2. _____   3. _____

4. _____   5. _____   6. _____

C **Find the missing letters. Then write the word.**

1. ___ ___ ___ t ___   _____

2. ___ ___ ___ ___ d   _____

D **Write the spelling word that rhymes with the word pair.**

1. snore   more   _____

2. worn   torn   _____

3. birth   earth   _____

Name _____

© 2001 Steck-Vaughn Company. All Rights Reserved.

Words with *or*

world	bore	born
worth	snore	worn

A Fill in the boxes with the correct spelling words.

1.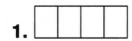

2.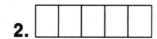

3.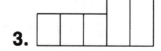

4.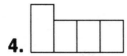

5.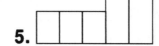

6.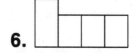

B Fill in each blank with the correct spelling word.

1. Write the two words that have the letters *orn*.

   _____   _____

2. Write the three words that begin with *w*.

   _____   _____   _____

3. Which two words end with *ore*? _____   _____

C Circle the word that is the same as the top one.

snore	world	worn	worth	bore	born
srone	worlb	wonr	worth	borc	borr
snore	morld	worn	wortn	bore	bonn
snone	world	morn	worfh	bone	born
snorc	wonld	warn	wonth	dore	dorn

Words with *or*

world	bore	born
worth	snore	worn

A Use each spelling word in a cursive sentence.

world

worn

worth

bore

snore

born

B Circle the vowels that are in the spelling words.

a   e   i   o   u

Which of these vowels is silent in the spelling words? _____

C Use the correct spelling words to complete the story.

Day by day, the _____ seems smaller. More

children are _____ each minute.

As our world becomes more crowded, we must take care of

Earth's land. We can't let it be _____ away. We

depend on having clean air and water. Our world is

_____ so much to all of us.

© 2001 Steck-Vaughn Company. All Rights Reserved.

Name _____

Words with *or*

world	bore	born
worth	snore	worn

A Put an *X* on the word that is <u>not</u> the same.

1. snore	snore	snore	snoce	snore
2. world	world	world	world	worlb
3. born	born	born	born	dorn
4. bore	bore	dore	bore	bore

B Use spelling words to complete the puzzle.

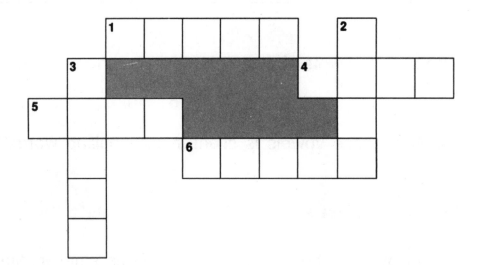

ACROSS

1. the earth

4. In what month were you ____?

5. used up

6. to make noises while asleep

DOWN

2. to make a hole

3. The party was

____ waiting for.

Words with *-oss* and *-ong*

toss	long	only
floss	strong	live

A Fill in each blank with a spelling word.

1. Did you see that boy _____ the softball?

2. I've been to the ocean _____ once.

3. The dentist told me to _____ my teeth every day.

4. It took me a _____ time to save the money.

5. The _____ woman lifted the box over her head.

6. How far do you _____ from the post office?

B Find the missing letters. Then write the word.

1. ___ ___ ___ o ___ ___   _____

2. ___ l ___ ___ ___   _____

3. ___ ___ ___ y   _____

C Write the spelling words in ABC order.

1. _____ 2. _____ 3. _____

4. _____ 5. _____ 6. _____

D Circle the letter that is the same in each spelling word.

toss   floss   long   strong

© 2001 Steck-Vaughn Company. All Rights Reserved.

Name _____

 **Words with *-oss* and *-ong***

toss	long	only
floss	strong	live

A Fill in the boxes with the correct spelling words.

1. 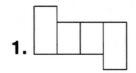   2. 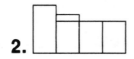   3.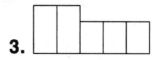

4. 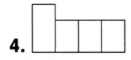   5. 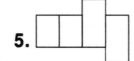   6.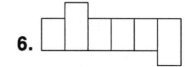

B Write each correct spelling word beside its clue.

_____ 1. This is a kind of thread for cleaning teeth.

_____ 2. This is the opposite of "short."

_____ 3. This means the same as "throw."

_____ 4. This means the opposite of "weak."

_____ 5. This word rhymes with "give."

C Put an *X* on the word that is <u>not</u> the same.

1. only	only	ohly	only	only
2. live	live	live	live	line
3. long	long	long	long	lomg
4. toss	tass	toss	toss	toss

Lesson 23

Words with *-oss* and *-ong*

toss	long	only
floss	strong	live

A Use each spelling word in a cursive sentence.

floss

long

toss

only

strong

live

B Circle the word that is the same as the top one.

floss	toss	long	strong	only	live
tloss	toss	lang	stromg	omly	liwe
flass	tass	lonq	strong	onlv	livc
floss	loss	lomg	sfrong	onty	live
floas	foss	long	stronq	only	leve

C Complete each sentence.

1. I <u>only</u> want _____.

2. Let's <u>toss</u> the _____.

3. I'd like to <u>live</u> where _____.

Name _____

© 2001 Steck-Vaughn Company. All Rights Reserved.

Words with *-oss* and *-ong*

toss	long	only
floss	strong	live

A Write a spelling word under each picture.

1. _____ 2. _____ 3. _____

B Write the spelling word that rhymes with the word pair.

1. cross   toss   _____

2. long   song   _____

3. floss   boss   _____

4. song   strong   _____

C Use the correct spelling words to complete the story.

Years ago, people who lived on the plains worked

_____ days. They didn't _____ near towns,

so they had to make what they needed. They grew their own

food. They made soap and sewed their own clothes.

Even the children had much work to do. Girls and boys

had to do farm work before they went to school. They had

_____ a short time each day for play.

Words with -*ew* and -*ue*

chew	due	head
drew	value	bread

A Fill in each blank with a spelling word.

1. The twins _____ their grandfather's advice.

2. The boy could turn cartwheels and stand on his _____.

3. Our puppy loves to _____ on our shoes.

4. We buy whole wheat _____ at the store.

5. My friend _____ the winning prize last night!

6. The airplane is _____ to land at 10:00 tonight.

B Fill in each blank with the correct spelling word.

1. Write the word that has two syllables. _____

2. Write two words that have a silent *a*.

   _____   _____

3. Write the shortest word. _____

C Circle the word that is the same as the top one.

chew	drew	due	value	head	bread
cheu	drew	dwe	walve	heab	bread
chew	dreu	dew	valeu	haed	brede
clew	dnew	due	value	lead	breod
chiw	brew	dve	valwe	head	dread

© 2001 Steck-Vaughn Company. All Rights Reserved.

Name _____

Words with *-ew* and *-ue*

chew	due	head
drew	value	bread

A Put an **X** on the word that is <u>not</u> the same.

1. drew	drew	dnew	drew	drew
2. value	value	value	value	valne
3. bread	bread	bread	bnead	bread

B Fill in the boxes with the correct spelling words.

1.

2.

3.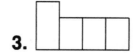

4.

5.

6.

C Use each spelling word in a cursive sentence.

due

value

drew

chew

head

bread

Words with -*ew* and -*ue*

chew	due	head
drew	value	bread

A Use the correct spelling words to complete the story.

I went to my first soccer practice yesterday. The coach

_____ plans of what he wanted us to do. Then we

played on the field.

It felt funny to hit the ball with my _____. My legs

were sore from running up and down the soccer field.

B Find the missing letters. Then write the word.

1. ____ r ____ ____ ____   _____

2. ____ r ____ ____   _____

3. ____ ____ ____ ____ e   _____

4. ____ h ____ ____   _____

5. ____ u ____   _____

C Fill in each blank with the correct spelling word.

1. Write the words that end with the letter *d*.

   _____   _____

2. Write the words that end with the letters *ue*.

   _____   _____

© 2001 Steck-Vaughn Company. All Rights Reserved.

Name _____

Words with -*ew* and -*ue*

chew	due	head
drew	value	bread

A Write the spelling words in ABC order.

1. _____ 2. _____ 3. _____

4. _____ 5. _____ 6. _____

B Find each hidden word from the list.

dew	chew	lead	due	clue	brew
few	slew	read	hue	blue	crew
hew	flew	bread	rue	true	drew
mew	blew	dread	sue	flue	grew
new	spew	tread	glue	value	
pew	stew	head	cue		

```
f  l  u  e  b  c  b  c  h  e  w  d
l  d  r  e  a  d  l  u  b  l  e  w
e  l  u  f  t  r  u  e  g  v  g  g
w  e  e  h  r  f  e  w  j  a  l  r
k  a  s  p  e  w  l  t  c  l  u  e
m  d  u  n  a  p  n  o  q  u  e  w
h  u  e  r  d  u  e  g  p  e  w  s
e  t  v  c  r  e  w  e  s  t  e  w
a  w  d  b  r  e  w  t  o  d  a  y
d  r  e  w  m  e  w  h  e  w  x  y
r  e  a  d  z  s  l  e  w  b  c  d
f  g  d  e  w  h  b  r  e  a  d  j
```

Words with *-ace*, *-ice*, and *-tion*

face	ice	station
space	price	location

A Fill in each blank with a spelling word.

1. The gas _____ has self-service pumps.

2. Can you tell me the _____ of these shoes?

3. He had to _____ the punishment for stealing the money.

4. It takes about two hours to freeze water into _____.

5. Where is the _____ of the party?

6. The rocket blasted into outer _____.

B Write each correct spelling word beside its clue.

_____ 1. This word has two syllables.

_____ 2. This word has a long *i* and five letters.

_____ 3. This is the shortest word.

C Fill in the boxes with the correct spelling words.

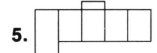
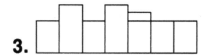

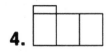
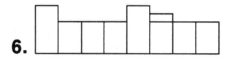

© 2001 Steck-Vaughn Company. All Rights Reserved.

Name _____

DAY 2

Words with *-ace, -ice,* and *-tion*

| face | ice | station |
| space | price | location |

A Circle the word that is the same as the top one.

station	ice	face	location	space	price
stafion	icc	facc	loeation	sgace	brice
statior	iec	face	locafion	sqace	price
station	ice	faee	locatior	space	pnice
statiom	iee	tace	location	spaec	priee

B Write the spelling word that rhymes with the word pair.

1. price mice _____

2. station nation _____

3. grace space _____

4. spice ice _____

C Write the spelling words that have two or more syllables.

_____   _____

D Find the missing letters. Then write the word.

1. ____ p ____ ____ ____   _____

2. ____ ____ ____ e   _____

3. ____ ____ i ____ ____   _____

Words with *-ace*, *-ice*, and *-tion*

DAY 3

face	ice	station
space	price	location

A Use each spelling word in a cursive sentence.

location

price

face

station

space

ice

B Write the spelling words in ABC order.

1. _____ 2. _____ 3. _____

4. _____ 5. _____ 6. _____

C Write each correct spelling word beside its clue.

_____ 1. This word means "the place where something is."

_____ 2. When something is for sale, this tells you how much it costs.

_____ 3. This is where your eyes, nose, and mouth are.

_____ 4. This is what will form when you freeze water.

© 2001 Steck-Vaughn Company. All Rights Reserved.

Name _____

Lesson 25 **Words with** *-ace, -ice,* **and** *-tion*

face	ice	station
space	price	location

A Write a spelling word under each picture.

1. _____   2. _____   3. _____

B Put an *X* on the word that is <u>not</u> the same.

1.	price	price	price	pirce	price
2.	station	station	statoin	station	station
3.	location	location	location	location	locotion
4.	face	face	face	face	faec
5.	space	space	space	sgace	space

C Use the correct spelling words to complete the story.

Have you ever been to a _____ camp? You can learn about rockets, planets, and space travel. The _____ of one such camp is in Maine. I've always wanted to go there. But the _____ for a week at this camp is very high.

You should have seen how happy I was when my parents said I could go!

110

Review

world	born	toss
worth	worn	floss
bore	strong	arrow
snore	long	narrow
ice	price	only

A **Write a spelling word under each picture.**

1. _____ 2. _____ 3. _____

4. _____ 5. _____ 6. _____

B **Fill in each blank with a spelling word.**

1. She is the _____ neighbor within two miles.

2. In which season were you _____?

3. The drill _____ into the piece of wood.

4. The jean jacket looked old and _____.

5. The long hike up the cliff was _____ it.

6. The trail was steep and _____.

7. Do you _____ when you sleep?

Name _____

© 2001 Steck-Vaughn Company. All Rights Reserved.

 **Review** _____

hear	chew	face
clear	drew	space
deer	due	station
steer	value	location
head	bread	live

C **Write the spelling word that rhymes with the word pair.**

1. nation   location   _____

2. head   dread   _____

3. space   race   _____

4. bread   tread   _____

5. face   place   _____

D **Use the correct spelling words to complete the story.**

Once my friend and I went camping in the mountains. The

_____ of the campground was beautiful. There was a

stream and many tall pine trees. During the day, we could

_____ birds singing. At night the sky was very

_____. We could see hundreds of stars. While hiking

on a trail, we saw a female _____. The deer looked at

us, and we could see her big brown eyes. Then she walked

away and began to _____ on some grass.

Words with -*dge* and -*ance*

edge	fudge	dance
hedge	judge	chance

A Fill in each blank with a spelling word.

1. The leaves on the tree seemed to _____ in the wind.

2. His uncle makes the best _____ I've ever eaten.

3. The _____ gave the blue ribbon to the youngest girl.

4. Have you ever had a _____ to go skiing?

5. The branches of the _____ need trimming.

6. If I look over the _____, I feel dizzy.

B Write the spelling words in ABC order.

1. _____   2. _____   3. _____

4. _____   5. _____   6. _____

C Fill in the boxes with the correct spelling words.

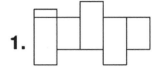

1.

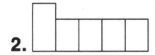

2.

3.

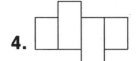

4.

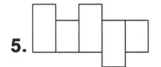

5.

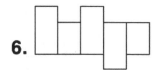

6.

© 2001 Steck-Vaughn Company. All Rights Reserved.

Name _____

Lesson 26

Words with -*dge* and -*ance*

edge	fudge	dance
hedge	judge	chance

A Use each spelling word in a cursive sentence.

edge _____

hedge _____

chance _____

fudge _____

dance _____

judge _____

B Find the missing letters. Then write the word.

1. ____ ____ n ____ ____   _____

2. j ____ ____ ____ ____   _____

3. f ____ ____ ____ ____   _____

C Fill in each blank with the correct spelling word.

1. Write the words that have the short *e* sound.

    _____   _____

2. Write the word that begins and ends with the same sound.

    _____

3. Write the word that begins and ends with the same letter.

    _____

DAY 3

Words with *-dge* and *-ance*

edge	fudge	dance
hedge	judge	chance

A Write the spelling word that rhymes with the word pair.

1. ledge   hedge   _____

2. glance   dance   _____

3. smudge   fudge   _____

B Circle the word that is the same as the top one.

edge	chance	hedge	dance	fudge	judge
ebge	chanec	hedeg	bance	tudge	jwdge
edge	chamce	hadge	dance	fndge	jubge
edgr	chance	ledge	damce	fubge	judge
edeg	cnance	hedge	danoe	fudge	iudge

C Write a spelling word under each picture.

1. _____   2. _____   3. _____

4. _____   5. _____

© 2001 Steck-Vaughn Company. All Rights Reserved.

Name _____

115

Words with -*dge* and -*ance*

edge	fudge	dance
hedge	judge	chance

A Make new words. Drop the *e*. Then add *ing*.

1. judge + ing = _____

2. dance + ing = _____

3. edge + ing = _____

B Circle the letters that are the same in each spelling word.

edge   hedge   fudge   judge

C Write each spelling word three times in cursive.

hedge _____

fudge _____

dance _____

chance _____

D Use the correct spelling words to complete the story.

A boy took something that didn't belong to him. He had to

go to court. The _____ heard his story and said she

would give him a second _____. He could work with

people who needed help. He promised he would never again

take something that did not belong to him.

Words with *age* and *igh*

age	light	high
cage	bright	sigh

A Fill in each blank with a spelling word.

1. The _____ from the sun hurts my eyes.

2. What is your _____?

3. The race car driver gave a _____ when her car would not start.

4. The bird flew out of the _____.

5. The full moon is very _____ tonight.

6. The house sat _____ on the hill.

B Find the missing letters. Then write the word.

1. h ____ ____ ____ _____

2. ____ ____ ____ e _____

3. ____ ____ ____ ____ t _____

C Fill in the boxes with the correct spelling words.

1.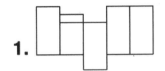

2.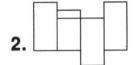

3.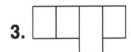

4.

5.

6.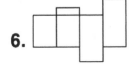

Name _____

© 2001 Steck-Vaughn Company. All Rights Reserved.

Words with *age* and *igh*

age	light	high
cage	bright	sigh

A Use each spelling word in a cursive sentence.

bright _____

cage _____

light _____

high _____

age _____

sigh _____

B Write a spelling word under each picture.

1. _____   2. _____   3. _____

C Write the spelling word that matches its antonym (opposite).

1. dull _____

2. low _____

3. dark _____

4. open place _____

5. youth _____

DAY 3

Words with *age* and *igh*

age	light	high
cage	bright	sigh

A Write the spelling word that rhymes with the word pair.

1. nigh   sigh   _____

2. might   light   _____

3. page   cage   _____

4. sight   bright   _____

B Fill in each blank with the correct spelling word.

1. Write the words that have a long *a* sound.

   _____   _____

2. Write the words that have a silent *g*.

   _____   _____

   _____   _____

3. If you remove the *c* from "cage," the new spelling word is

   _____.

4. The longest word is _____.

C Write the spelling words in ABC order.

1. _____   2. _____   3. _____

4. _____   5. _____   6. _____

Name _____

© 2001 Steck-Vaughn Company. All Rights Reserved.

Words with *age* and *igh*

age	light	high
cage	bright	sigh

A Put an *X* on the word that is <u>not</u> the same.

1.	cage	cage	caqe	cage	cage
2.	high	high	high	high	higk
3.	age	age	age	agc	age
4.	light	light	light	lighf	light
5.	sigh	sigh	sihg	sigh	sigh
6.	bright	bright	bright	bright	birght

B Circle the letters that are the same in each spelling word.

light   bright   high   sigh

C Use the correct spelling words to complete the story.

I had always wanted a pet. So when I was ten years old,

my parents bought a rabbit for me. I opened the

_____ and looked in. The rabbit's _____

eyes stared at me. She was white with black spots.

I could tell she was shy. I picked her up and stroked her

soft fur. She snuggled against my shirt. I knew we were

going to be friends. She lived to the _____ of seven.

Words with *ugh*

brought	caught	though
thought	taught	through

A Fill in each blank with a spelling word.

1. I _____ a bad cold and had to stay in bed.

2. We will go camping, even _____ it looks like rain.

3. He _____ his new football to the party and showed everyone how to throw it.

4. Do you think we can go _____ the hallway?

5. She _____ the little girl how to use the tools.

6. Have you _____ about what you will wear to the game?

B Fill in the boxes with the correct spelling words.

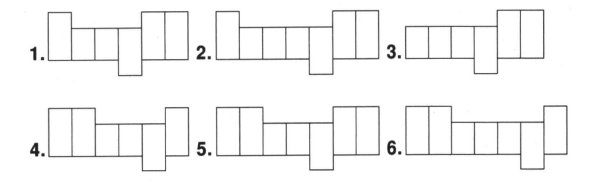

1.

2.

3.

4.

5.

6.

C Write the spelling words that have *ough* in them.

_____   _____

_____   _____

© 2001 Steck-Vaughn Company. All Rights Reserved.

Name _____

121

Lesson 28

Words with *ugh*

brought	caught	though
thought	taught	through

A Circle the word that is the same as the top one.

caught	though	brought	taught	thought	through
caughf	thuogh	brought	faught	toughf	throuqh
caught	thouhg	brouhgt	taught	thonght	thnough
canght	thongh	bnought	tanght	thougkt	through
cauqht	though	drought	tuaght	thought	fhrough

B Use the correct spelling words to complete the story.

An otter is _____ by its mother to swim fast. The water is its home. _____ it moves much faster in water, it can move on land.

It is _____ that the otter is one of the most playful of animals. They love to build slides on the banks of streams and slide down them again and again.

C Write a spelling word under each picture.

1. _____   2. _____   3. _____

Words with *ugh*

brought	caught	though
thought	taught	through

A Use each spelling word in a cursive sentence.

thought _____

brought _____

taught _____

caught _____

though _____

through _____

B Find the missing letters. Then write the word.

1. c ___ ___ ___ ___   _____

2. t ___ ___ ___ ___ t   _____

3. ___ ___ r ___ ___ ___ ___   _____

C Write each correct spelling word beside its clue.

_____ **1.** "Threw" is a homonym for this word.

_____ **2.** This word means "carried."

_____ **3.** This word can mean "an idea."

_____ **4.** This word can mean "helped someone learn."

_____ **5.** This word ends in a long *o* sound.

© 2001 Steck-Vaughn Company. All Rights Reserved.

Name _____

DAY
4

Words with *ugh*

brought	caught	though
thought	taught	through

A Write the spelling words in ABC order.

1. _____ 2. _____ 3. _____

4. _____ 5. _____ 6. _____

B Use spelling words to complete the puzzle.

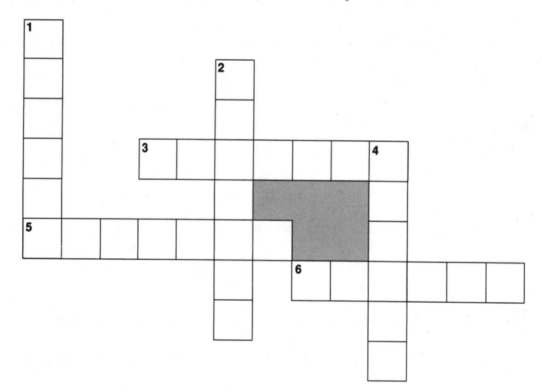

ACROSS

3. I _____ you a snack.

5. among or between

6. Who _____ you how to swim?

DOWN

1. trapped

2. past tense of "to think"

4. while, or however

Lesson 29

DAY 1

Words with *sc-*, *kn-*, and *wr-*

scene	knee	write
science	known	wrinkle

A **Fill in each blank with a spelling word.**

1. He hurt his _____ playing hockey.

2. Do you _____ with your left or right hand?

3. She was in one _____ in the play.

4. A funny smell can make you _____ your nose.

5. Do you like to do _____ experiments?

6. How long have you _____ that you won the prize?

B **Fill in the boxes with the correct spelling words.**

1.

2.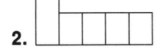

3.

4.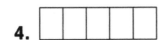

5.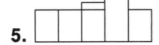

6.

C **Write a spelling word under each picture.**

1. _____   2. _____   3. _____

Name _____

125

© 2001 Steck-Vaughn Company. All Rights Reserved.

Words with *sc-*, *kn-*, and *wr-*

scene	knee	write
science	known	wrinkle

A Use each spelling word in a cursive sentence.

scene

science

knee

known

write

wrinkle

B Find the missing letters. Then write the word.

1. ____ c ____ ____ ____   _____

2. ____ ____ ____ ____ n   _____

C Fill in each blank with the correct spelling word.

1. Write the two words that have a silent *k*.

   _____   _____

2. Write the three words that have a silent *w*.

   _____   _____   _____

3. Write the two words that have a silent *c*.

   _____   _____

Words with *sc-*, *kn-*, and *wr-*

scene	knee	write
science	known	wrinkle

A Write the spelling words in ABC order.

1. _____ 2. _____ 3. _____

4. _____ 5. _____ 6. _____

B Write the five spelling words that have long vowel sounds.

_____   _____

_____   _____

_____

C Circle the word that is the same as the top one.

scene	science	knee	known	write	wrinkle
sceme	scienec	knee	knewn	write	wrimkle
senee	sciencc	knec	knowm	wnite	wrinkle
scene	science	kuee	hnown	wrile	wrinhle
sceue	seicnce	hnee	known	writc	wrinlke

D Complete each sentence.

1. I like to <u>write</u> about _____.

2. I hit my <u>knee</u> on the _____.

Name _____

© 2001 Steck-Vaughn Company. All Rights Reserved.

Words with *sc-*, *kn-*, and *wr-*

scene	knee	write
science	known	wrinkle

A Use the correct spelling words to complete the story.

My sister thinks she's getting old. She worries too much.

Each time she sees a _____ on her face, she

sighs and makes a big _____. I think she's acting

silly. After all, she's only 23 years old.

B Find each hidden word from the list.

scene	wrong	wrench	write	knew	knee
scenery	wrap	wreck	wring	knock	knelt
scent	wreath	wrestle	wrinkle	know	kneel
science	wren	wrist	wrote	known	

```
b  c  k  n  e  e  d  f  w  a  s  h  g
w  r  i  t  e  w  r  e  a  t  h  s  w
r  s  h  j  k  r  l  w  m  n  s  c  r
a  c  p  k  n  e  w  r  q  r  c  e  o
p  i  s  c  i  s  s  o  r  s  e  n  t
s  e  c  t  v  t  k  n  o  w  n  t  e
k  n  e  e  l  l  w  g  w  r  e  c  k
x  c  p  y  s  e  k  n  o  w  r  e  n
z  e  t  w  r  e  n  c  h  w  y  b  o
s  c  e  n  e  c  e  w  r  i  n  g  c
d  w  r  i  n  k  l  e  f  s  g  h  k
w  r  i  s  t  j  t  k  l  h  m  n  p
```

Words with *-ard* and *-irt*

beard	dirt	could
board	skirt	every

A Fill in each blank with a spelling word.

1. Will you wear the red or the black _____?

2. My younger brother loves to play in the _____.

3. Can you jump off the diving _____?

4. If he doesn't shave, he'll grow a _____.

5. She said I _____ go with them to the concert.

6. Brush your teeth after _____ meal.

B Circle the word that is the same as the top one.

beard	skirt	board	dirt	could	every
beand	shirt	doarb	dint	coold	evrey
bearb	skirt	boand	drit	coudl	every
beard	skint	board	brit	could	eveny
bcard	skirf	baord	dirt	coulb	euery

C Find the missing letters. Then write the word.

1. ____ ____ ____ l ____   _____

2. ____ o ____ r ____   _____

3. ____ ____ ____ ____ y   _____

© 2001 Steck-Vaughn Company. All Rights Reserved.

Name _____

Words with -*ard* and -*irt*

beard	dirt	could
board	skirt	every

A Fill in the boxes with the correct spelling words.

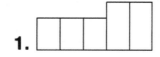 1.

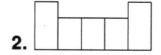 2.

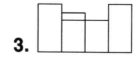 3.

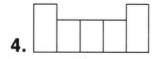 4.

5.

6.

B Put an *X* on the word that is <u>not</u> the same.

1.	skirt	skirt	skirt	skirf	skirt
2.	board	board	board	board	boand
3.	dirt	dirt	dirt	drit	dirt
4.	beard	beard	deard	beard	beard
5.	every	every	every	evevy	every
6.	could	could	coulb	could	could

C Write the spelling words in ABC order.

1. _____ 2. _____ 3. _____

4. _____ 5. _____ 6. _____

DAY 3

Words with *-ard* and *-irt*

beard	dirt	could
board	skirt	every

A Use each spelling word in a cursive sentence.

beard _____

board _____

skirt _____

dirt _____

every _____

B Use the correct spelling words to complete the story.

I _____ spend all my time learning from nature.

_____ leaf, rock, and shell tells a story. Nature is a

great teacher.

Even _____ holds many clues about the past. If

you look carefully, you may find proof of life long ago.

Fossils and shells can be found in unlikely places.

C Write a spelling word under each picture.

1. _____ 2. _____ 3. _____

Name _____

© 2001 Steck-Vaughn Company. All Rights Reserved.

Words with *-ard* and *-irt*

beard	dirt	could
board	skirt	every

A Complete each sentence with a spelling word.

1. The word "dirt" rhymes with _____.

2. Hair growing on a man's face is called a _____.

3. The word that has a silent *l* is _____.

4. The word that is a homonym for "bored" is _____.

B Find each hidden word from the list.

yard	cord	skirt	hurt	beard	squirt
hard	port	shirt	spurt	board	lard
short	flirt	blurt	herd	third	card
fort	dirt	curt	heard	bird	

```
b  h  u  r  t  o  r  v  s  t  b  b
h  i  o  p  h  a  r  d  q  x  l  i
e  p  r  c  i  l  p  o  r  t  u  r
a  s  m  a  r  t  q  k  c  o  r  d
r  m  y  r  d  z  u  p  s  a  t  s
d  b  a  d  o  h  i  s  h  r  s  q
a  e  r  w  m  e  r  h  o  d  s  u
r  a  d  h  o  r  t  i  r  s  k  i
d  r  t  d  k  d  o  r  t  p  i  r
m  d  a  f  l  i  r  t  c  u  r  t
d  i  r  t  f  o  r  t  o  r  t  o
l  a  r  d  b  o  a  r  d  t  w  k
```

Review

edge	dance	light
hedge	science	bright
fudge	age	high
judge	cage	sigh
dirt	skirt	could

A Write a spelling word under each picture.

1. _____ 2. _____ 3. _____

4. _____ 5. _____ 6. _____

B Fill in each blank with a spelling word.

1. She said she _____ help me with my work.

2. I will sweep the _____ off the floor.

3. They keep their pet bird in a _____.

4. He trimmed the _____ in his front yard.

5. The light from the lamp was very _____.

6. I gave a loud _____ when I lost the game.

7. The _____ was dressed in a black robe.

Name _____

© 2001 Steck-Vaughn Company. All Rights Reserved.

Review

brought	scene	write
thought	chance	wrinkle
caught	knee	board
taught	known	beard
though	through	every

C Write the spelling word that rhymes with the word pair.

1. dance   prance   _____

2. bite   kite   _____

3. free   bee   _____

4. own   sown   _____

5. crinkle   sprinkle   _____

D Use the correct spelling words to complete the story.

It's fun to act in a play. I like to take a _____ from a

play and make it come alive with my voice and my body. A

teacher _____ me how to show feelings with my face.

Just a wrinkle in my nose makes a difference. We go

_____ many practices to get a scene right. When it's

time to perform, I know _____ line. Even _____

I sometimes mess up, it is wonderful to be on stage. I love to

hear people clap at the end of the show.

Words I Can Spell

Put a ✓ in the box beside each word you spell correctly on your weekly test.

1

- [ ] bee
- [ ] free
- [ ] feet
- [ ] meet
- [ ] once
- [ ] your

2

- [ ] peach
- [ ] heat
- [ ] clean
- [ ] beans
- [ ] read
- [ ] give

3

- [ ] law
- [ ] draw
- [ ] how
- [ ] plow
- [ ] clown
- [ ] frown

4

- [ ] oil
- [ ] spoil
- [ ] coin
- [ ] join
- [ ] joy
- [ ] toy

5

- [ ] scout
- [ ] trout
- [ ] cloud
- [ ] proud
- [ ] ground
- [ ] pound

Words To Review

If you miss a word on your test, write it here. Practice it until you can spell it correctly. Then check the box beside the word.

Name _____

© 2001 Steck-Vaughn Company. All Rights Reserved.

Words I Can Spell

Put a ✓ in the box beside each word you spell correctly on your weekly test.

6

☐ real   ☐ speak

☐ deal   ☐ dream

☐ beak   ☐ leap

7

☐ paid   ☐ trail

☐ wait   ☐ plain

☐ mail   ☐ brain

8

☐ broom   ☐ spoon

☐ groom   ☐ tool

☐ moon   ☐ cool

9

☐ boat   ☐ coast

☐ throat   ☐ load

☐ toast   ☐ road

10

☐ blade   ☐ snake

☐ shade   ☐ scale

☐ flake   ☐ whale

Words To Review

If you miss a word on your test, write it here. Practice it until you can spell it correctly. Then check the box beside the word.

_____

_____

_____

_____

_____

_____

_____

_____

_____

_____

_____

_____

_____

_____

Words I Can Spell

Put a ✓ in the box beside each word you spell correctly on your weekly test.

Words To Review

If you miss a word on your test, write it here. Practice it until you can spell it correctly. Then check the box beside the word.

—— 11 ——

☐ cane   ☐ grape
☐ pane   ☐ base
☐ scrape   ☐ case

—— 12 ——

☐ plate   ☐ flame
☐ state   ☐ pave
☐ tame   ☐ brave

—— 13 ——

☐ glide   ☐ wife
☐ pride   ☐ bike
☐ life   ☐ strike

—— 14 ——

☐ mile   ☐ grime
☐ while   ☐ vine
☐ dime   ☐ spine

—— 15 ——

☐ ripe   ☐ bite
☐ stripe   ☐ drive
☐ wise   ☐ why

Name _____

© 2001 Steck-Vaughn Company. All Rights Reserved.

Words I Can Spell

Put a ✓ in the box beside each word you spell correctly on your weekly test.

16

- ☐ code
- ☐ rode
- ☐ joke
- ☐ broke
- ☐ home
- ☐ know

17

- ☐ pole
- ☐ stone
- ☐ slope
- ☐ rose
- ☐ note
- ☐ drove

18

- ☐ hold
- ☐ cold
- ☐ snow
- ☐ throw
- ☐ own
- ☐ don't

19

- ☐ fair
- ☐ chair
- ☐ care
- ☐ spare
- ☐ share
- ☐ stare

20

- ☐ far
- ☐ scar
- ☐ dark
- ☐ shark
- ☐ art
- ☐ start

Words To Review

If you miss a word on your test, write it here. Practice it until you can spell it correctly. Then check the box beside the word.

_____

_____

_____

_____

_____

_____

_____

_____

_____

_____

_____

_____

_____

_____

_____

_____

My Word List

Words I Can Spell

Put a ✓ in the box beside each word you spell correctly on your weekly test.

21

- ☐ hear
- ☐ clear
- ☐ deer
- ☐ steer
- ☐ arrow
- ☐ narrow

22

- ☐ world
- ☐ worth
- ☐ bore
- ☐ snore
- ☐ born
- ☐ worn

23

- ☐ toss
- ☐ floss
- ☐ long
- ☐ strong
- ☐ only
- ☐ live

24

- ☐ chew
- ☐ drew
- ☐ due
- ☐ value
- ☐ head
- ☐ bread

25

- ☐ face
- ☐ space
- ☐ ice
- ☐ price
- ☐ station
- ☐ location

Words To Review

If you miss a word on your test, write it here. Practice it until you can spell it correctly. Then check the box beside the word.

_____
_____
_____
_____
_____
_____
_____
_____
_____
_____
_____
_____
_____
_____
_____
_____

Name _____

© 2001 Steck-Vaughn Company. All Rights Reserved.

Words I Can Spell

Put a ✓ in the box beside each word you spell correctly on your weekly test.

Words To Review

If you miss a word on your test, write it here. Practice it until you can spell it correctly. Then check the box beside the word.

26
- ☐ edge
- ☐ hedge
- ☐ fudge
- ☐ judge
- ☐ dance
- ☐ chance

27
- ☐ age
- ☐ cage
- ☐ light
- ☐ bright
- ☐ high
- ☐ sigh

28
- ☐ brought
- ☐ thought
- ☐ caught
- ☐ taught
- ☐ though
- ☐ through

29
- ☐ scene
- ☐ science
- ☐ knee
- ☐ known
- ☐ write
- ☐ wrinkle

30
- ☐ beard
- ☐ board
- ☐ dirt
- ☐ skirt
- ☐ could
- ☐ every

Word Study Sheet

(Make a check mark after each step.)

Name _____

Words	1 Look at the Word	2 Say the Word	3 Think About Each Letter	4 Spell the Word Aloud	5 Write the Word	6 Check the Spelling	7 Repeat Steps (if needed)

© 2001 Steck-Vaughn Company. All Rights Reserved.

Graph Your Progress

(Color or shade in the boxes.)

Number of words correctly spelled:

	Lesson 1	Lesson 2	Lesson 3	Lesson 4	Lesson 5	Lesson 6	Lesson 7	Lesson 8	Lesson 9	Lesson 10	Lesson 11	Lesson 12	Lesson 13	Lesson 14	Lesson 15	Lesson 16	Lesson 17	Lesson 18	Lesson 19	Lesson 20	Lesson 21	Lesson 22	Lesson 23	Lesson 24	Lesson 25	Lesson 26	Lesson 27	Lesson 28	Lesson 29	Lesson 30
6																														
5																														
4																														
3																														
2																														
1																														

Name _____